Erscheint nur das alte graue Gestein.
Wenn der Bogen Trümmer schwarz in der Nacht
Und weithin schimmert der Fenster Pracht,
Wenn der kalte Dunstguß, schwankend, erhellt,
Auf das Mittelthürmchen
Wenn Pfeiler um Pfeiler aus hohe Ruinen fällt;
bald Ebenholz schimmern, bald Elfenbein;
Wenn das Bildwerk hervortritt als Silbergestein
Und die Sprüche von Lebens Vergänglichkeit!
Wenn der Tweed von fern zischt brausend
Und die Eule schreit über des Todten Grab
Dann gehe doch geh allein hinaus —
Und sieh St. Davids altes Haus,
Und schwöre bei der Wiederkehr
Dir schien keine Trauer so schön.

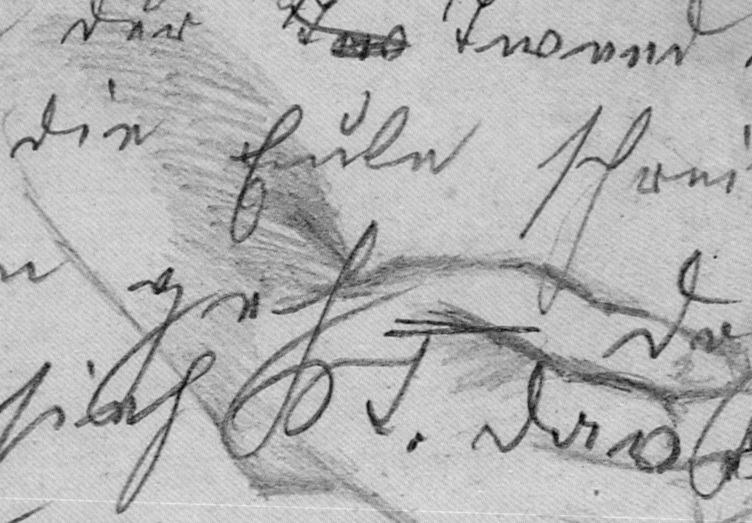

W. RAPHAEL

THE CANADIAN ART LIBRARY

William Raphael

LIFE & WORK

By Pierre-Olivier Ouellet

This book was made possible thanks to the generous support of its benefactors.

SEASON SPONSOR, 2025–2026 PUBLICATIONS
POWER CORPORATION OF CANADA

PRESENTING SPONSOR
JONATHAN WENER, CM

TITLE SPONSORS
ALAN AND PATRICIA KOVAL FOUNDATION
THE SCHULICH FOUNDATION
THE JACK WEINBAUM FAMILY FOUNDATION

GOLD SPONSOR
THE MORRIS & ROSALIND GOODMAN FAMILY FOUNDATION

SILVER SPONSORS
THE AZRIELI FOUNDATION
THE DELANEY FAMILY FOUNDATION
THE DH GALES FAMILY CHARITABLE FOUNDATION
THE SPATZ FOUNDATION

CONTRIBUTORS
TAMARA FINE AND DARREN SUKONICK
PETER AND NERI SLAN
THE WEISZ FAMILY

Contents

Fig 1 William Raphael, *Sunset*, n.d., oil on cardboard, 23 x 35 cm, Musée de Lachine, Montreal.

Introduction

In his early twenties, before leaving Prussia for Quebec, William Raphael anglicized his name from Israel Rafalsky. For an unknown painter to assume the moniker of a famed Renaissance genius was a startling act of *chutzpah*—one that foreshadowed his noteworthy career as the first Jewish professional artist in Canada, a painter whose work would end up in museums across his adopted country, and a creative talent whose story deserves attention.

Despite Raphael's celebrated beginning, it would take more than a century for this book, the first major account of the artist's life, to be published. Although he was respected enough by his peers to have been appointed to nascent academies in late nineteenth-century Canada, sought after as a teacher, and collected across the country, apart from references to his work in Dennis Reid's *A Concise History of Canadian Painting* (1988), Raphael has—until now—received scant art historical attention.

With erudition and scholarly insight, Pierre-Olivier Ouellet rectifies this oversight, which is crucial to our understanding of Canadian art. This book shares the remarkable story of how, when Raphael arrived in Montreal in October 1857, there were no resident portrait painters in the city. Prepared to prove that he was the man for the job, he came armed with examples of his art created in Europe. It didn't take long before the city took note of his talents. Within a year of his arrival, Raphael had completed twelve commissions.

His portraits, however, were just the start. As he established himself in Montreal, where he and his wife raised nine children, he set his sights on documenting his adopted home with a vitality and energy that would leave a lasting record of life in pre-Confederation Quebec. His works, including *Haymarket Square / Victoria Square*, 1861 (fig. 60), and *Behind Bonsecours Market, Montreal*, 1866 (fig. 63), introduced Canadians to the Biedermeier style, with their emphasis on realism, genre scenes, and celebration of everyday people and places.

As early as the 1870s, Raphael painted the habitants of New France wearing woven coloured *ceintures fléchées* and winter toques, in modest interiors. These scenes would be echoed in the works of artists who followed in his footsteps, including Marc-Aurèle de Foy Suzor-Coté (1869–1937) and Alfred Laliberté (1877–1953).

As Ouellet explains in the following pages, Raphael's legacy is important and noteworthy. Along with his contemporaries Cornelius Krieghoff (1815–1872) and James Duncan (1806–1881), he was one of the first artists to explore the theme of Canada's northern winter identity. Long before such painters as Maurice Cullen (1866–1934), Clarence Gagnon (1881–1942), and A.Y. Jackson (1882–1974) were documenting the country's terrain, Raphael, as Ouellet tells us, "recognized the strong role Canada's northern landscape played in defining the country."

In addition to depicting the emerging nation, Raphael had a key part to play in professionalizing the visual arts and training the next generations of creators. When he opened his own studio in 1866, he presented himself as an artist and a teacher. Raphael became a founding member of both the Society of Canadian Artists and the Canadian Academy of Arts (later renamed the Royal Canadian Academy of Arts), organizations that worked to formalize the exhibition and promotion of the visual arts in Canada.

Despite his considerable accomplishments, Raphael's career success did not shield him from artistic, political, and social tensions that arose at the turn of the twentieth century in Montreal. As a result, his name and his pioneering work were left out of history.

A renewed attention to Raphael's art came in 2015, when over 150 years after his arrival in Quebec, the artist once again made history. At a Christie's auction in London, a vigorous bidding war took place for the painting *Bonsecours Market, Montreal*, 1880 (fig. 25), a later counterpart to *Behind Bonsecours Market, Montreal*. The National Gallery of Canada, which already owned the earlier work, purchased the later painting for more than $400,000 (hammer price), an amount that exceeded the modest estimate of $37,400 to $56,100. The bid set a landmark sales record for the artist and brought fresh reverence for Raphael and his importance.

While it took an auction in England to spark a resurgence of interest in Raphael, one Montreal collector has been carrying the torch for the painter since the 1970s. Jonathan Wener, the artist's great-great-grandson, first came to know Raphael's work when he saw it hanging in his grandmother's home as a child.

Although history had not been kind to Raphael, Wener was compelled to collect his art, fascinated by what it revealed about the people, origins, and identity of Canada. After he saw *Behind Bonsecours Market, Montreal* at the National Gallery of Canada, twenty-year-old Wener acquired a reproduction and set out on a journey—more than five decades long—to acquire his great-great-grandfather's art and build a collection of over 160 works.

This publication is a testament to Wener's tenacity, which laid a foundation for the scholarship of Ouellet. It is with thanks to their commitment and shared vision that this volume, the first critical study of Raphael's oeuvre, has been possible. It is with appreciation to them both that an artist who had the strength and confidence to voyage to a new country that he then helped build and grow now has a well-earned and well-documented place in history.

Sara Angel CM, PHD
Founder and Executive Director, Art Canada Institute
November 2025

Biography

Fig 2 William Raphael, *The Rafalsky family home in Nakel*, May 6, 1851, watercolour and graphite on wove paper, 15.8 x 10 cm, National Gallery of Canada, Ottawa.

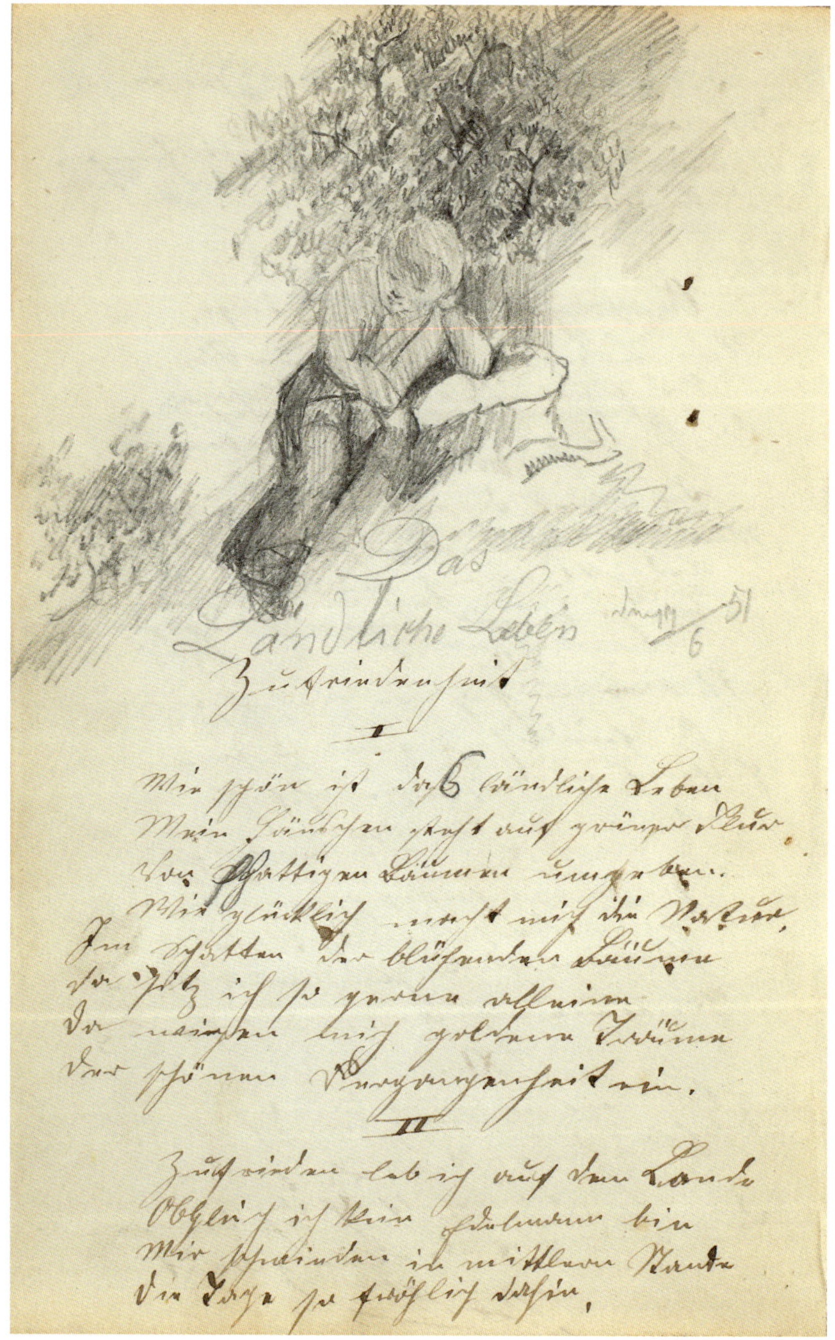

Fig 3 William Raphael, Manuscript of poem entitled *Das Ländliche Leben* (*Life in the Country*), July 6, 1851, graphite on wove paper, 15.8 x 10 cm, National Gallery of Canada, Ottawa.

The first Jewish artist to forge a professional career in Canada, William Raphael played a vital role in shaping the country's artistic landscape. Born in 1833 in Eastern Europe and trained in Berlin, Raphael chose to exile himself in Montreal, where his genre scenes—rich in realism and rooted in local life—captured a growing nation in transition. Beyond the canvas, he left his mark as a teacher and as a founding figure of two major institutions: the Art Association of Montreal and the Royal Canadian Academy of Arts. But a tide of anti-Semitism that swept the globe clouded Raphael's legacy and ultimately drove him to withdraw from the art world before his death in 1914.

Early Years and Artistic Training

William Raphael was born Israel Rafalsky in Prussia on August 22, 1833. One of several children of Paulena Samuel (1805–1852) and Wolf Rafalsky (1796–1856), he was raised in an Orthodox Jewish household in the town of Nakel (present-day Nakło nad Notecią in Poland) (fig. 2). During Raphael's youth, this region in Eastern Europe was an important centre for the Haskalah, or Jewish Enlightenment, a movement that encouraged the modernization of Jewish communities through exposure to more secular education and culture. Raphael benefited from this time of reform. He was educated in three languages—German, Hebrew, and Yiddish[1]—and in 1850, he took his first lessons on the violin.[2] Along with music, Raphael studied Romantic poetry and ancient history, broadening his cultural pursuits.[3] At a very early age, he also began drawing and taking notes in his sketchbooks, a habit he kept up throughout his life (fig. 3–10).

On August 3, 1851, the eve of his eighteenth birthday, Raphael left his family home to pursue formal artistic training at the Royal Prussian Academy of Arts in Berlin.[4] Although the school's archives have no record of his enrolment—as many documents were destroyed during the Second World War[5]—Raphael's notebooks from the period confirm that he did indeed pay his tuition fees in September 1851.[6] The school boasted several teachers who were well known in Berlin society at the time, including portraitists Johann Eduard Wolff (1786–1868), Carl Joseph Begas (1794–1854),[7] and Friedrich Wilhelm Heinrich Herbig (1788–1861)[8] and landscape painter Ferdinand Konrad Bellermann (1814–1889). It's likely that Raphael was influenced by several of these teachers as he began to develop his own artistic identity.

As part of his academic training, Raphael was exposed to two great models prevalent in European art schools in the nineteenth century: nature and antiquity.[9] His notebooks contain drawings of live models and representations of figures from Greco-Roman antiquity (fig. 6). Other sketches from this period focus on human anatomy.[10] In one, for example, Raphael reproduces a flayed figure by French sculptor Edmé Bouchardon (1698–1762) (fig. 10–11). He also created small studies of human body parts, such as an oil painting of a hand. These were the types of exercises that students in the academic system were expected to complete.

Unfortunately, this period in Berlin was marked by several deaths in Raphael's family: first his mother in 1852; then his sisters Kalah and Bertha in 1853 and 1854; and finally his father in 1856.[11] These events, combined with a population boom and fierce competition for jobs in Prussia, prompted Raphael to leave Europe and settle in North America.[12] The young artist took care to draw sketches of his friends and family before his departure.[13] Among his meagre belongings were a few works that would demonstrate his artistic skills, including some portraits he'd painted in 1855. *Portrait of a Woman* (fig. 12), dated June 8, captures the subject looking over her shoulder. While playing with strong contrasts of light and dark, Raphael shows great talent for depicting the woman's face. Note the artist's signature on the bottom left of this

Fig 4 William Raphael, *Sketchbook No. 3*, 1853–76, sketchbook containing forty-seven drawings in graphite, pen, and brown ink on thirty-six leaves of wove paper, bound in brown imitation-leather covers, cover, 17.3 x 11.5 cm, National Gallery of Canada, Ottawa.

Fig 5 William Raphael, *Old Woman Sitting on Curb*, April 23, 1856, pen, brown ink, watercolour, and graphite on wove paper, 20.1 x 11.6 cm, National Gallery of Canada, Ottawa.

Fig 6 William Raphael, *Study after Antinous*, 1851–56, graphite on wove paper, 15.8 x 10 cm, National Gallery of Canada, Ottawa.

Fig 7 William Raphael, *Berlin, 1853*, December 11, 1853, pencil on sketchbook paper, 20.3 x 12.5 cm, collection of Jonathan Wener, Montreal.

Fig 8 William Raphael, *Man Posing in a Kneeling Position*, c.1851–56, pencil on paper, 12.5 x 20.3 cm, collection of Jonathan Wener, Montreal.

Fig 9 William Raphael, *Two Women*, 1852, pencil on paper, 12.5 x 20.3 cm, collection of Jonathan Wener, Montreal.

Fig 10 William Raphael, after Edmé Bouchardon, *Study of a Nude Male Sculpture*, 1854, graphite on wove paper, 20.1 x 11.6 cm, National Gallery of Canada, Ottawa.

Fig 11 Edmé Bouchardon, *Flayed* (*Écorché*), 1760, plaster, dissection cast, and metal, 208 x 70 x 60 cm, École des Beaux-Arts, Paris.

Fig 12 William Raphael, *Portrait of a Woman*, June 8, 1855, oil on cardboard, 36.1 x 29 cm, Musée de Lachine, Montreal.

Fig 13 Currier & Ives, New York (publisher), *The Steam-ship "Borussia" (screw-propeller). Regular packet between Hamburg and New York*, c.1857–72, colour lithograph, 33 x 18 cm, The Mariners' Museum and Park, Newport News, Virginia.

Fig 14 William Raphael, *Sinking of the Schooner* Industry, December 19, 1856, graphite on paper, 8.5 x 14.1 cm, collection of Jonathan Wener, Montreal.

work, which confirms that by the 1850s, he had already changed his name from Israel Rafalsky to William Raphael.

Raphael crossed the Atlantic from Hamburg to New York aboard a pioneering steamship, the *Borussia* (fig. 13), whose maiden voyage had taken place just a few months earlier.[14] The ship left port on December 2, 1856, but the crossing was disrupted by bad weather and a collision with a schooner, the *Industry*, on the night of December 19.[15] Raphael produced two drawings of the scene, showing the schooner gradually sinking into the ocean (fig. 14). The captain and crew were rescued and taken aboard Raphael's ship.[16] Three days later, the *Borussia* docked in New York.[17] Knowing only a few words of English but with the names and addresses of various acquaintances in hand, Raphael stayed in the city for a few months.[18] On April 21, 1857, he left the United States by train to join his brother Meier Rafalsky, also known as Morris Raphaelsky (1825–1914), in Montreal.[19]

Starting Out in Montreal

Although his brother Meier relocated to St. Louis, Missouri, in October 1857,[20] young William Raphael found Montreal a favourable place to establish himself (fig. 15). At the time, there were no resident portrait painters in the city; it was mostly served by itinerant artists travelling from place to place. In fact, only the Irish-born James Duncan (1806–1881) had made his home in Montreal, where he painted landscapes and genre scenes.[21]

Armed with the portraits that had crossed the Atlantic with him, Raphael soon managed to convince several prominent Montrealers of his talents. Members of the Silvermann family were the first to call on him,[22] and commissions followed regularly from that point on. Like his contemporary Paul Kane (1810–1871), who also began his career as a portraitist,[23] Raphael produced a substantial number of works, completing twelve commissions before the end of 1857. In 1858, he carried on at this prolific pace in Montreal, while also travelling to Quebec City to meet other clients.[24]

Raphael's portraits brought him to the attention of photographer William Notman (1826–1891). Notman had arrived in Montreal from Scotland in 1856 and opened a photographic studio at a time when this new medium—with its low cost and its ability to produce images quickly and easily—was enjoying great success. Even though the city already had a well-established daguerreotypist in T.C. [Thomas Coffin] Doane (1814–1896),[25] Notman readily obtained numerous commissions and won several awards for his daguerreotypes and ambrotypes. He also counted on the support of the Montreal bourgeoisie and produced portraits of members of the city's most prominent families (fig. 16). Notman offered his clients portraits finished with oils or watercolours (fig. 17).[26] The success of his business combining photography with painting allowed him to hire a variety of artists, including the Scottish-born painter Charles Smeaton (1838–1868). In 1859, he called on the services of William Raphael.[27] This was a productive collaboration that resulted in many fine portraits, including one of Sir William Fenwick Williams, then commander-in-chief of the British forces in the

Fig 15 Portrait of William Raphael, c.1865, photographer unknown, collection of Jonathan Wener, Montreal.

Fig 16 (LEFT) William Notman Studio, *Hugh Andrew Montagu Allan, Montreal, Quebec, 1866–1867*, 1866–67, albumen print, 9 x 5.5 cm, McCord Stewart Museum, Montreal. **Fig 17** (RIGHT) William Notman Studio and John Arthur Fraser (painter), *Master Hugh Allan, Montreal, QC, 1867*, 1867, silver salts and watercolour on card, albumen process, 69 x 52 cm, McCord Stewart Museum, Montreal. **Fig 18** (OPPOSITE PAGE) William Raphael, *The Old Pedlar*, 1859, oil on canvas, 76.3 x 89.1 cm, Art Gallery of Nova Scotia, Halifax.

colony. The portrait was temporarily exhibited at the Quebec stock exchange building in December 1859 and was described by the Quebec *Morning Chronicle* newspaper as "admirable" and "life-like."[28]

Raphael continued his work with Notman's studio into the following year, as evidenced by an article in the *Montreal Herald* newspaper published on August 27, 1860,[29] as well as a few portraits dated that same year.[30] But by 1861, the business relationship was over, as Raphael himself noted to the press in 1886.[31] His work with Notman had guaranteed him a stable income, but the end of the partnership offered Raphael the opportunity to pursue a personal practice focused on genre scenes.

Raphael began to produce works with many of the hallmarks of the Biedermeier style, an artistic movement that seems to have influenced his creative vision during his formative years in Berlin. With its emphasis on realism, Biedermeier aimed to depict subjects from everyday life. This was the context for Raphael's piece *The Old Pedlar* (fig. 18), painted in July 1859. In September, the work was on display at Dawson & Sons, a prominent local firm selling books and stationery. Benjamin Dawson and his sons, Samuel Edward and William Valentine, were among the city's most active cultural figures at the time. Their store was also one of the few places where photographs and paintings were exhibited and offered for sale, often in books illustrated with engravings.[32] Here, Raphael's *The Old Pedlar* did not go unnoticed. The *Montreal Herald* and *Daily Commercial Gazette* published some very positive lines on the subject:

> A good painting is on view at Messrs. Dawson & Sons. The subject is the interior of a [peasant woman's] humble dwelling with several figures, the principal one being a pedlar, no doubt in the fancy hardware line from the contents of his basket. He has just effected the sale of a looking-glass, and with open hand he is waiting to receive the ready for it.... All the figures seem full of life and feeling, even the dog, who is cautiously making up to the pedlar, is in true character.[33]

The scene is described in detail, with the journalist praising the artist's ability to create an original composition and capture the expressions that animate the characters. The writer also explicitly highlights the painter's identity, telling readers, "The picture, a local production, has been supposed to be a copy, but it is really an original from the easel of W. Raphael, an Artist from the Berlin Academy, at present at Mr. Notman's Studio."[34] With this article, Raphael began to gain recognition in his adopted city. From this point on, he inscribed "Montreal" in full on many of his paintings.

On December 17, 1859, in a sign of the painter's increasing activity, the *Morning Chronicle and Commercial and Shipping Gazette* critiqued four works on display at the Quebec stock exchange building, including one entitled *The School* and a self-portrait (fig. 21).[35] Then, in August 1860, Raphael's latest creation, an allegorical painting entitled *Union of Europe and America*, was featured as part of the festivities around the visit of the Prince of Wales to Montreal. The iconography of this painting is unique in the artist's repertoire. "Its design was a figure of Brittania, with a mural crown," reported

Fig 19 (OPPOSITE PAGE) William Raphael, *Boy and a Cart*, 1860, oil on canvas, 58.4 x 47 cm, collection of Jonathan Wener, Montreal. **Fig 20** Cornelius Krieghoff, *Merrymaking*, 1860, oil on canvas, 88.9 x 121.9 cm, Beaverbrook Art Gallery, Fredericton.

the *Montreal Herald*, "placing wreaths on the heads of a female figure representing Europe, and a male one in Indian costume, representing America, both mounting the steps to a throne."[36] A transparency of the work was illuminated in the evenings in Jacques Cartier Square, undoubtedly to the delight of spectators.

In this period, Raphael continued his personal work, focusing on genre scenes depicting the Canadian people and landscape and significant places in the city. Some of the paintings from this time, such as *Haymarket Square / Victoria Square*, 1861 (fig. 60), feature the Montreal haymarket. Others, such as *Boy and a Cart* (fig. 19), 1860, and *Going to Town* (fig. 129), 1862, show figures on horse-drawn sleighs or carts. Many of Raphael's pieces from this period, including *Royal Mail, New Brunswick* (fig. 125), 1861, reflect the northern character of the British colony, calling to mind the work of Cornelius Krieghoff (1815–1872) (fig. 20).

Raphael began his career during a period of artistic renewal in Montreal. Between 1858 and 1860, several foreign painters established themselves in the city, contributing to a more fertile cultural environment. Among these were the English-born artists C.J. Way (1835–1919) and John Arthur Fraser (1838–1898). Fraser later became a valued employee of William Notman's. Similarly, in 1860, landscape painter Otto Reinhold Jacobi (1812–1901), a fellow Prussian, decided to make Montreal his home, as did animal painter Adolphe Vogt (1842–1871) in 1865.[37]

As Montreal's population swelled to 90,323 in 1861,[38] it began to attract a growing number of art lovers and collectors who supported cultural initiatives such as a public art exhibition held at Bonaventure Hall in the summer of 1857.[39] But the city was still without a permanent art museum and art school. To address the lack of official infrastructure for artists, members of the city's intellectual and financial elite took the lead in forming a professional arts association. The first meeting of a group of twenty-three English-speaking gentlemen, including Anglican bishop Francis Fulford, was at the home of William Notman on January 11, 1860. Only two painters, C.J. Way and William Raphael, were invited to take part in the project.[40] Barely two weeks later, the group had established the foundation for what would later be called the Art Association of Montreal. According to art historian Jean Trudel, the association's aims were to "build up and present a permanent collection of paintings and sculptures, organize temporary exhibitions and a program of animation, and create a specialized public library and a school of fine arts."[41] As a founding member, Raphael was a regular participant in the association's activities, both its expositions and its *conversazione* (private evening discussions reserved for distinguished guests).[42]

As he forged personal and professional relationships in the Montreal art scene, Raphael also became involved in the city's small Jewish and German-speaking community. He painted portraits of some of its members, including Mr. Hermann Danziger in August 1857.[43] Perhaps this is when Raphael first met Danziger's daughter, Ernestina (1844–1925), with whom he became romantically involved.[44] It's unclear how this relationship began, but by 1861, according to the Canadian census, Raphael was living at the Danziger home at 63½ German Street.[45] He courted the

Fig 21 William Raphael, *Self-Portrait*, 1862, oil on canvas mounted on cardboard, 47.6 x 25.6 cm, collection of Jonathan Wener, Montreal.

young woman under the watchful eye of members of the Danziger family and eventually asked her to marry him. Before their union was announced, the young couple were photographed separately by William Notman in 1862, each posing in an identical setting, perhaps on the same day (fig. 22–23). On October 29, 1862, their wedding was celebrated by the well-known rabbi Abraham de Sola at the Spanish and Portuguese Synagogue of Montreal.[46] The couple had the first of their nine children, a son they named Rudolph, in 1863.

Major Achievements

In January 1863, Montreal photographer Abner Bedee Taber (1832–1866) offered William Raphael a one-year contract to paint portraits based on his photographs.[47] A Taber advertisement in the Montreal directory boasted that the painter was "well known as a first-class artist."[48] This offer guaranteed Raphael a regular income—he received fifteen dollars and thirty-eight cents every Saturday from the photographer[49]—which he could use to finance the production of speculative works for the Montreal market.[50] In the second half of the nineteenth century, the city's art market consisted mainly of auctions or exhibitions of works in bookshops and framing stores. Raphael relied on the occasional support of Dawson & Sons and gallery owner William Scott (1831–1904) to buy or sell his paintings.[51]

The artist also began making more ambitious compositions depicting urban life. One of these creations, entitled *Bonsecours Market*, was included in the second exhibition organized by the Art Association of Montreal (AAM) in February 1864.[52] Raphael's work, which was shown alongside paintings by Cornelius Krieghoff, Robert Scott Duncanson (1821–1872), and even J.M.W. Turner (1775–1851), won high praise at the *conversazione* held at the opening of the event, and that praise was echoed in the *Montreal Herald*:

> An extremely clever picture was sent by Mr. Raphael, a young Canadian artist. The subject was a very characteristic street scene in front of the Bonsecours Market in the height of the early morning business in the winter time. The figures are full of life and animation, and the costumes, the carriages, the snow, and the winter atmosphere just after sunrise, are all rendered, with remarkable happiness and faithfulness. This is a genuine Canadian picture in every sense of the word.[53]

In the eyes of connoisseurs and critics, Raphael—now identified in the press as a "Canadian artist" rather than a student of the Berlin Academy—had produced a work that was his first major achievement.[54] Although the 1864 painting has been lost, a drawing from the same year gives us insight into the composition of this winter scene (fig. 24). Raphael also produced a variation of the painting sixteen years later, in 1880, which allows us to better grasp its full significance (fig. 25). The later work captures the hustle and bustle of a busy street full of temporary stalls lined up against the facade of the Bonsecours Market. In both pieces, the scene is framed by distinctive

Fig 22 (LEFT) William Notman, *Miss Danziger, Montreal, QC, 1862*, 1862, silver salts on paper mounted on paper, albumen process, 8.5 x 5.6 cm, McCord Stewart Museum, Montreal. **Fig 23** (RIGHT) William Notman, *William Raphael, artist, Montreal, QC, 1862*, 1862, silver salts on paper mounted on paper, albumen process, 8.5 x 5.6 cm, McCord Stewart Museum, Montreal.

Fig 24 William Raphael, *Bonsecours Market*, 1864, graphite, ink, watercolor, and white highlights, 24.1 x 29.8 cm, private collection.

Fig 25 William Raphael, *Bonsecours Market, Montreal*, 1880, oil on canvas, 30.4 x 40.7 cm, National Gallery of Canada, Ottawa.

Fig 26 William Raphael, *Arrocher*, 1865, graphite on paper, 17.5 x 24.9 cm,McCord Stewart Museum, Montreal.

Fig 27 William Raphael, *Fireside Chat in the Clearing*, 1867, oil on canvas, 61 x 106.7 cm, collection of Jonathan Wener, Montreal.

Fig 28 Robert S. Duncanson, *Land of the Lotus Eaters*, 1861, oil on canvas, 134 x 225 cm, the Royal Palace, Stockholm, Sweden.

Montreal landmarks, including the high dome of the market and the steeple of Notre-Dame-de-Bon-Secours Chapel.

Raphael's professional success most likely prompted his father-in-law, Hermann Danziger, to introduce him to the closed circle of Freemasonry in April 1864.[55] Through this family connection, Raphael was able to enter the ranks of this secret society, which in turn made it possible for him to broaden his social and cultural circle. He certainly met members of the upper class who were willing to commission him to paint their portraits.

Raphael also continued his own practice, presenting a painting at the AAM's third exhibition, which opened on February 27, 1865.[56] That summer, he took a short trip to Scotland, during which he added various drawings, including *Arrocher*, 1865, to his notebooks (fig. 26). His reasons for going to Scotland remain unknown. From this journey, he produced only one painting, depicting Loch Achray and Ben Venue mountain, in 1869.[57] On his return to Canada, Raphael rented his family's first home, a few steps away from his in-laws' house, at 98 German Street—a street that, as its name suggests, was mainly populated by German-speaking Canadians.[58] The family remained at this address until 1887.[59]

In his new home, he began work on a composition set behind the Bonsecours Market (fig. 63). A preparatory painting was presented at the Montreal Provincial Exhibition in the fall of 1865. Although the work won him first prize for an oil painting,[60] some newspapers condemned the caricatured appearance of the figures in the scene and took the opportunity to ridicule the artist's surname: the Montreal painter was, according to the critics, no match for the great Renaissance master Raphael (1483–1520). Although stung by these remarks, Raphael created a larger version of the Bonsecours Market scene in 1866, adding a detail that visually countered the petty comments of the critics.

In the 1860s, Raphael's works were rooted in local reality, sometimes with a humorous edge, but he also tackled more imaginative themes. Some paintings from this period feature unusual encounters inspired by marginal characters (such as fortune tellers and tarot readers) and set in vast landscapes, as in *Fireside Chat in the Clearing*, 1867 (fig. 27). Perhaps influenced by the African American painter Robert Scott Duncanson, who showed his 1861 work *Land of the Lotus Eaters* (fig. 28) in Montreal in 1863 and 1864,[61] Raphael seems to have let his mind wander to more fanciful images. Like Duncanson, who was associated with the Hudson River School, Raphael opts for a panoramic format, bathing the landscape in late-day light while the mountains in the background seem to disappear. Also like Duncanson, he populates the scene with characters who seem to have sprung from the imagination, or even from another era. One of his compositions produced in this vein earned him a favourable review in London's *Art Journal*.[62] Although this encouraged him to continue this approach for some time, he abandoned it in the early 1870s (fig. 29–31).

Fig 29 William Raphael, *An Afternoon in the Woods*, 1866, oil on canvas, 55.9 x 91.4 cm, collection of Jonathan Wener, Montreal.

Fig 30 William Raphael, *In the Mirror*, 1870, 31.1 x 24.1 cm, collection of Jonathan Wener, Montreal.

Fig 31 William Raphael, *An Afternoon in the Woods* (detail), 1866, oil on canvas, 55.9 x 91.4 cm, collection of Jonathan Wener, Montreal.

Fig 32 William Raphael, *Habitants Attacked by Wolves*, 1870, oil on canvas, 60.3 x 160 cm, Montreal Museum of Fine Arts.

Fig 33 William Raphael, *Boating at Dusk*, 1878, oil on canvas, 41.3 x 31.1 cm, collection of Jonathan Wener, Montreal.

Teaching and Shaping the Nation's Art

William Raphael opened his own studio in 1866, in a space at 147 rue Saint-Jacques. As reported in the city directory, he presented himself as both an "artist and teacher of figure & landscape painting."[63] In fact, over the next few years, Raphael was as committed to teaching the arts as he was to advancing his own painting career. At a time when no Montreal institution offered training in the fine arts, the young painter found many people eager to learn artistic techniques and to develop the ability to judge works, part of the cultural veneer expected in Victorian society.[64] Perhaps to better serve his students, Raphael moved his studio four times between 1867 and 1877. But he always made sure he remained at the centre of urban activity, choosing spaces on rue Saint-Jacques and Place d'Armes.[65] In 1878, he moved his studio again—this time to 193 rue Saint-Pierre, a space he kept until around 1883.[66]

In addition to launching his teaching career, Raphael joined the Society of Canadian Artists, which was founded by John Arthur Fraser in 1867. He became one of the first members of this organization, whose primary aim was to promote the work of local artists at the dawn of Confederation.[67] Within this group, Raphael joined the ranks of significant painters such as Frederic Bell-Smith (1846–1923), James Duncan, Allan Edson (1846–1888), and Henry Sandham (1842–1910). Despite the society's short-lived existence (it shut down in 1873), Raphael took part in its first two exhibitions. He exhibited a total of five works, including two paintings that were later distributed more widely via chromolithography.

The painting entitled *The Early Bird Picks Up the Worm*, shown at the first exhibition in 1868, was reproduced by chromolithographers Roberts & Reinhold in 1869 (fig. 67). The following year, *Habitants Attacked by Wolves* (fig. 32), unveiled at the second exhibition, was reproduced by Burland & Lafricain.[68] In both cases, the prints received good reviews in the press and met certain cultural expectations. In the 1860s, chromolithography was embraced by many amateur collectors and connoisseurs, who viewed it as a process that perfectly imitated watercolours and oil paintings.[69] This means of reproduction made Raphael's art more affordable and more widely available to a general audience.

From the mid-1860s to the early 1870s, while still teaching, Raphael began to diversify his thematic repertoire by producing landscapes (fig. 33–36). With the growth of the railroads, he made numerous summer trips, discovering new places to include in works like *Boating at Dusk*, 1878 (fig. 33). In addition to recording drawings in his notebooks, he produced *plein air* sketches to better capture outdoor scenes (fig. 35–36). He spent the summer of 1869 in the Charlevoix region, travelling from Murray Bay to Cap-à-l'Aigle, and was very enthusiastic about these places, which had to that point been relatively unknown to painters. "Mr. Raphael speaks in high terms of a district which may well be called the Switzerland of Canada," the *Quebec Daily Mercury* reported, "and which will yet be the favorite sketching ground of the artists of America."[70] Drawings such as *Cap-à-l'Aigle*, made in August 1878, are reminders that he continued to travel and record his impressions in his sketches (fig. 35).

Fig 34 William Raphael, *Pointe-au-Pic, Murray Bay—Approaching Storm*, 1878, oil on cardboard, 28.3 x 45.5 cm, collection of Jonathan Wener, Montreal.

Fig 35 William Raphael, *Cap-à-l'Aigle*, August 3, 1878, graphite on wove paper, 9.4 x 14.6 cm, National Gallery of Canada, Ottawa.

Fig 36 William Raphael, *Falaise à Murray Bay*, 1887, oil on cardboard, 25.1 x 39.4 cm, collection of Jonathan Wener, Montreal.

Fig 37 William Raphael, *Habitant Warming*, c.1872–1910, oil on canvas, 35.5 x 27.9 cm, collection of Jonathan Wener, Montreal.

Fig 38 William Raphael, *Coachman Standing at Rest Smoking a Pipe*, 1881, oil on canvas, 50.8 x 40.6 cm, collection of Jonathan Wener, Montreal.

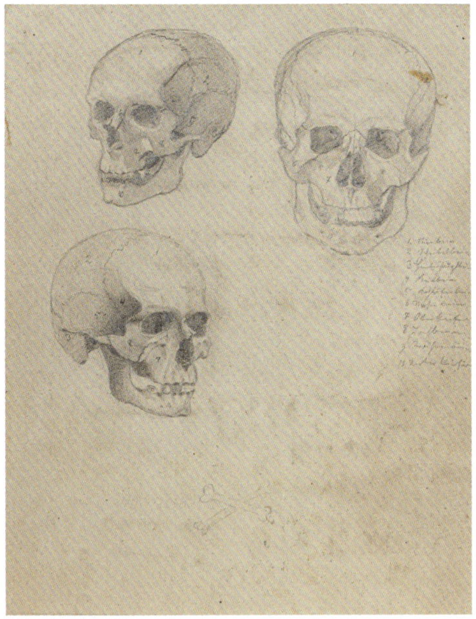

Fig 39 (LEFT) William Raphael, *Study of a Human Skull*, 1851–56, graphite on paper, 83.5 x 57.5 cm, collection of Dr. Stevenson Strobel, Toronto. **Fig 40** (RIGHT) William Raphael, *Pack of Wolves*, c.1879, charcoal on paper, 31.5 x 57 cm, McCord Stewart Museum, Montreal.

In addition to landscapes, Raphael increasingly turned his attention to depicting local characters, particularly the figure of the habitant (fig. 37). For example, *Habitant (or Preparing to Smoke)*, c.1872–1910 (fig. 79), is a typical composition: the figure is depicted in a closed, windowless room, alone and near a stove. From 1872 onward, Raphael created many scenes featuring the habitant, as well as different variations, such as *Coachman Standing at Rest Smoking a Pipe*, 1881 (fig. 38).

Despite an economic crisis that raged in the West starting in 1873,[71] Raphael continued his activities and, presumably to ensure a certain income, accepted various commissions for portraits. These included a series of seven family portraits painted in the mid-1870s of Dr. Louis-Édouard Desjardins; his wife, Zaïde Paré; their respective parents; and an uncle, Father Joseph-Octave Paré, canon of the Montreal cathedral. The *Portrait of Louis-Édouard Desjardins*, 1877 (fig. 135), bears a striking resemblance to a photograph published in 1875 in a book by the Reverend J. Douglas Borthwick.[72] At the time, photography was becoming an increasingly popular tool for painters like Raphael, who could use photographs, rather than preparatory sketches, as accurate references.

Raphael also began receiving requests from members of Montreal's medical community. At the end of the 1870s, for example, Dr. William Osler commissioned him to depict organs and various pathologies to illustrate Osler's articles and supplement his teaching.[73] Though medical illustration was only a short-lived endeavour for the artist, it was nevertheless a rare opportunity for him to build upon skills he had developed during his training in Berlin, where he often made sketches depicting human anatomy, such as skulls and leg muscles (fig. 39).

A Cornerstone of Canadian Art

In 1879, following a generous bequest from the well-known art collector Benaiah Gibb, the Art Association of Montreal (AAM) opened its first permanent pavilion in Phillips Square, ushering in a new era in Canadian art.[74] As an accomplished artist with a well-established reputation, William Raphael was naturally included in the exhibition held at the building's inauguration in May 1879. Attended by the governor general of Canada, the Marquess of Lorne (John Campbell, 1845–1914), and his wife, Princess Louise (1848–1939), it was one of the city's most prestigious events.[75] Several European paintings were displayed alongside works by Canadian artists like Henry Sandham, James Duncan, Daniel Fowler (1810–1894), and Thomas Mower Martin (1838–1934). Raphael exhibited an oil painting entitled *Habitants Pursued by Wolves*.[76] The work cannot be located today, but a charcoal drawing called *Pack of Wolves*, c.1879 (fig. 40), preserved at the McCord Stewart Museum, may be a preparatory study.

Also in 1879, building on his ties to the arts community, Raphael became a member of the Ontario Society of Artists (OSA), an association founded seven years earlier by John Arthur Fraser.[77] Membership allowed him to take part in the group's annual exhibition, held in Toronto in September of that year. He presented four paintings, including the ambitious landscape *Indian Encampment on the Lower St. Lawrence Estuary*,

Fig 41 Homer Watson, *The Pioneer Mill*, 1880, oil on canvas, 86 x 127.8 cm, Royal Collection Trust, Windsor Castle, Berkshire.

1879 (fig. 84).[78] The exhibition was covered in several newspapers because of a visit from the Marquess of Lorne,[79] and also because it gave rise to a project to form a royal academy of arts in Canada.[80] Seizing the opportunity, Lucius R. O'Brien (1832–1899), the vice-president of the OSA, drew up a constitution and gave the governor general the names of eight artists to be considered as the first academicians. The select group included William Raphael (who became a naturalized Canadian in 1872),[81] indicating the high esteem in which he was held.[82]

With the official inauguration of the Canadian Academy of Arts on March 6, 1880 (it took the name Royal Canadian Academy of Arts in 1882),[83] Raphael became one of the founding academicians.[84] His large composition *Indian Encampment on the Lower St. Lawrence Estuary* was accepted as a reception piece.[85] The ambitious nightscape, depicting the high cliffs of Cap-Blanc, was also part of the academy's first exhibition, which opened at Ottawa's Clarendon Hotel on March 8. The painting was additionally reproduced in the April 10 edition of the *Canadian Illustrated News*, alongside three other works presented at the first exhibition.[86] The pieces were accompanied by a few words that captured the public's intense interest in the academy:

> [W]e publish to-day a few of the diploma pictures which figured at the late Exhibition of the Canadian Academy of Arts at Ottawa. In almost every respect, this first test Exhibition was a success, testifying to the ability of our native artists, and giving the very best reply to the croakers who pretended that the country was not aesthetically prepared for so important an institution.[87]

The governor general's support for the arts in Canada was reaffirmed when it was announced that he had purchased six works from the exhibition for his personal collection, including a painting by Homer Watson (1855–1936) (fig. 41), another by Fraser, three works by O'Brien, and a painting by William Raphael.[88] Raphael's piece, *L'Habitant (The Habitant)*, received a rave review in *Rose-Belford's Canadian Monthly and National Review*, which called it "simply perfect."[89]

The accolades and high-profile support encouraged Raphael to invest in the new institution. He became one of the first members of its board, took part in various meetings, and made sure to participate in its annual exhibitions.[90] In 1882, he was even named a member of the organizing committee for the next exhibition, to be held in Montreal, sharing the honour with Napoléon Bourassa (1827–1916), Thomas Mower Martin, and William Nicoll Cresswell (1818–1888).[91] He continued to play a constant role in Montreal's artistic development, which included accepting an invitation in 1879 to teach painting to the Sisters of Sainte-Anne congregation.[92] This helped him establish links with the community, which then engaged him to create some religious works for the chapel.[93]

Raphael's stellar reputation and his fifteen years of experience as a teacher made him an obvious candidate when the Art Association of Montreal began looking for someone to oversee a series of courses the organization wanted to offer at its new

Fig 42 (LEFT) William Notman & Sons, *Art Association Building, Phillips' Square, Montreal, QC*, c.1893, silver salts on paper mounted on paper, albumen process, 20.3 x 25.4 cm, McCord Stewart Museum, Montreal.
Fig 43 (RIGHT) Georges-Édouard-Amable Desbarats, after William Raphael, *Study of the Head of an Iroquois Chief, Caughnawaga*, 1881, McGill Libraries, Rare Books and Special Collections, Montreal.

pavilion in Phillips Square (fig. 42). This initiative would allow the association to achieve one of its core objectives: to educate and train Canadian artists. At the end of 1880, the AAM hired Raphael and announced in the newspapers that three courses were now open for enrolment. According to the *Gazette*, one of those courses was "in figure painting and drawing, under the instruction of Mr. Raphael."[94] The other two courses were in composition and landscape painting, taught by Allan Edson (1846–1888), and modelling and sculpture, taught by François Van Luppen (1838–1899). Classes began in January 1881 and attracted forty-two students in all. Edson did not continue teaching the following autumn, and Raphael took over the composition and landscape course.

As these first classes were being offered, the AAM began work on a "portfolio containing ten autotype copies of original pictures,"[95] intended to be distributed to all its members. Printed in 1881 by George-Édouard Desbarats (1838–1893), the portfolio included pieces by Way, Edson, O'Brien, Fraser, and Sandham.[96] Raphael was the only artist to be represented twice, with *Scene at Murray Bay*, 1881, which offers a view of the majestic rocky cape similar to that found in *Indian Encampment on the Lower St. Lawrence Estuary*, and *Study of the Head of an Iroquois Chief, Caughnawaga*, 1881 (fig. 43).[97] The collection was a chance to promote not only Raphael's reputation but also his abilities as a teacher in figure and landscape painting.

As a leading player on the Montreal and broader Canadian art scene, Raphael was also invited by Lucius R. O'Brien to take part in the book *Picturesque Canada*, a kind of travelogue that would be richly illustrated with engravings. Four of his works were commissioned to be reproduced in the book, which was edited by George Monro Grant, rector of Queen's University in Kingston. Presumably because of his earlier work, Raphael was asked to create images for the section devoted to French Canadians. The pieces were *An Old Habitant* (based on an 1881 painting), *Habitant with Snowshoes* (fig. 44–45), and *Half-Breed Fisherman* (fig. 46–47). A final image, used at the start of the chapter, depicts a seated man with a pipe in his hand—a subject often taken up by the artist. The colossal work, published in 1882, had 880 pages and over 500 woodcuts in two leather-bound volumes and was one of the most sumptuous printed works to appear in Canada at the time.[98]

Tensions and Clashing Visions

William Raphael's career success did not shield him from the struggles that could emerge in the rather restricted artistic environment of the early 1880s. On the eve of his fiftieth birthday, he found himself immersed in various disputes that reflected the rise of anti-Semitism following the 1881 assassination of Tsar Alexander II—an event falsely blamed on the Jewish community. Anti-Jewish sentiment led not only to pogroms in Russia and Romania and to the scandalous Dreyfus affair in France,[99] but also to racial discrimination that emboldened the rhetoric of the most fearsome anti-Semites, including historian and journalist Goldwin Smith (1823–1910) in Toronto.

Fig 44 William Raphael, *Habitant with Snowshoes*, 1873, pencil and watercolour on paper, 22.9 x 15.2 cm, collection of Jonathan Wener, Montreal.

Fig 45 Edith Cooper, after William Raphael, *Habitant with Showshoes*, 1882, engraving published in *Picturesque Canada: The Country as It Was and Is* by George Monro Grant (Toronto: Belden, 1882), volume 1, page 67.

Fig 46 William Raphael, *Half-Breed Fisherman*, 1874, pencil and watercolour on paper, 24.1 x 15.2 cm, collection of Jonathan Wener, Montreal.

Fig 47 William Raphael, *Half-Breed Fisherman*, 1877, oil on canvas, 33 x 25.4 cm, collection of Jonathan Wener, Montreal.

Fig 48 (ABOVE) "South Kensington Museum: The Sculpture Hall," in *The Queen's London: A Pictorial and Descriptive Record* (London: Cassell & Co., 1896), page 171. **Fig 49** (BELOW) Robert Harris, *Self-Portrait*, 1910, oil on canvas, 77.2 x 61.1 cm, National Gallery of Canada, Ottawa.

Smith, who described Jews as "parasites,"[100] spread his racist ideas in the columns of many newspapers. He was one of several Canadian writers peddling anti-Jewish sentiment in the 1880s; others included John Wilson Bengough (1851–1923) in Toronto, through his magazine *Grip*,[101] and Jules-Paul Tardivel (1851–1905) in Quebec City, through his newspaper *La Vérité*.[102] Like some members of the clergy, these people helped to spread a negative view of Jews in Quebec and throughout Canada, and Smith's ideas in particular later strongly influenced several prominent politicians and statesmen, including Henri Bourassa, William Lyon Mackenzie King, and Vincent Massey.[103]

It was in this context that the Art Association of Montreal decided, in December 1882, not to renew William Raphael's appointment as a professor. The organization suspended classes for a few months, during which time the board of directors formed an arts education committee[104] and began to develop a new vision, taking as a model the art school at the South Kensington Museum in London (renamed the Victoria & Albert Museum in 1899) (fig. 48).[105] Strongly convinced of the supposed artistic superiority of this institution, the members of the AAM's education committee set about recruiting a British teacher. This approach was unsuccessful, and the association opted instead for a teacher from Montreal's English-speaking community who was familiar with the principles of academic training. In 1883, the AAM introduced portraitist Robert Harris (1849–1919) as its new—and only—teacher (fig. 49). Trained not in London but in Paris, Harris set out to duplicate the French Beaux-Arts model.

This professional blow did not prevent Raphael, now on the cusp of turning fifty, from continuing his artistic work and teaching. Perhaps as a response to the AAM's machinations, he chose to show a sketch depicting a student, in one of his popular *plein air* painting sessions, as part of the organization's spring 1883 exhibition (fig. 50).[106] It should be emphasized that this painting reflects an avant-garde teaching approach, indicating that Raphael was likely one of the first art teachers in Canada to give outdoor drawing and painting classes—many years before landscape painter William Brymner (1855–1925) followed suit.[107]

Raphael also continued to teach in several other places. In addition to giving classes to the nuns of Sainte-Anne, he became a professor of oil painting at the Montreal Society of Decorative Art.[108] In 1884, he was also recruited by Mrs. Lovell's Educational Institute,[109] an English-speaking Montreal school for the education of young girls. And he continued to offer painting and drawing lessons in his own studio, where he had been welcoming and training students for close to two decades.

His extensive involvement in arts education over the years prompted him to take steps to obtain funding for his studio. He applied to the Royal Canadian Academy of Arts (RCA), which has had a budget to support arts education in Canada since 1884. Raphael's applications that year and in 1885 failed to convince the board, however.[110] Faced with these successive rejections, he must have felt as if the Canadian art world—which had once welcomed him so warmly, and had even relied on his reputation at various foundational moments to achieve its goals—had suddenly turned its back on him.

Fig 50 William Raphael, *A Sketch from Nature*, October 5, 1882, oil on board, 25.4 x 20.3 cm, collection of Jonathan Wener, Montreal.

Fig 51 (LEFT) A modest sign on a pilaster in front of 1310 Sainte-Catherine Street, Montreal, indicates William Raphael's studio, c.1884–1910, photographer unknown, collection of Jonathan Wener, Montreal.
Fig 52 (RIGHT) William Brymner, *In the Orchard (Spring)*, 1892, oil on paperboard, 40.2 x 30.6 cm, National Gallery of Canada, Ottawa.

In 1884, Raphael relocated his studio to 1310 rue Sainte-Catherine,[111] not far from the AAM (fig. 51). His courses competed directly with those offered by the association. He placed numerous newspaper ads, in both the *Gazette* and the *Montreal Star*, to publicize his classes and recruit new students.[112] These were repeated the following year, in September and October, and every year after that until September 1908.[113] The AAM could not have been pleased by the success of William Raphael's studio, as reported in the newspapers of the day. On June 6, 1885, for example, the *Montreal Star* covered a drawing exhibition he'd organized and highlighted the work of his students, many of whom were associated with influential Montreal families, such as the Lighthalls, Lymans, Allans, and Morgans.[114] A few days later, Raphael himself was also singled out for praise by the *Gazette*:

> The first thought that comes to the beholder is that the teacher had undoubtedly impressed upon his pupils the duty of striving after truth above all things.... [The drawings exhibited are] a more praiseworthy proof of the instructor's tact and assiduity that, while aiding the innate gift of each of his pupils to unfold in its own way, he has been able to impart to them all a real appreciation of artistic truthfulness with the feeling for accuracy in technique.[115]

That year, Raphael had thirty students, according to the *Montreal Star*. This was an impressive number in comparison to the thirty-seven enrolled in the courses offered by Robert Harris at the AAM, which had superior premises and financial resources.[116]

In 1886, William Brymner succeeded Harris as course director. He continued teaching in the French academic tradition established by his predecessor.[117] That same year, the press began to question the supposed impartiality of the organizing committees of the AAM and RCA exhibitions.[118] Attention was called to the favouritism shown towards certain painters—especially Brymner, O'Brien, and Harris. The lack of financial transparency was also openly criticized, as was the authority of the AAM secretary, a Mr. English, who seemed to run the institution as he pleased.

As the AAM found itself embroiled in controversy, it attempted to divert attention to William Raphael. Mr. English made contemptuous and misleading remarks about him that were eventually reported in the newspaper : "Raphael, being a teacher, cannot be expected to paint, besides he never had any education except what he got in Notman's studio, painting photographs. All the pictures which he has sent to the gallery for the last few years have been failures."[119] Faced with this defamation, Raphael took to his pen to correct the facts. "For those of the public who may have been misled by the information received from this gentleman concerning me," he replied, "I may state that I was born and educated in Germany, that I was a student of the Royal

Fig 53 William Raphael, *Awaiting Mother's Return on a Snowy Day*, 1891, oil on canvas, 71.1 x 43.2 cm, collection of Jonathan Wener, Montreal.

Fig 54 William Raphael, *Two Women in Rowboat Near Shoreline*, July 5, 1911, oil on canvas, 30.5 x 43.2 cm, collection of Jonathan Wener, Montreal.

Fig 55 William Raphael, *The Artist's House in Victoria St.*, 1908, watercolour on paper, 26.7 x 31.8 cm, collection of Jonathan Wener, Montreal.

Fig 56 William Raphael, *The Artist's Dog Niny*, c.1895, oil on canvas, 30.5 x 40.6 cm, collection of Jonathan Wener, Montreal.

Academy of Berlin for nearly eight years uninterruptedly, and received a first-class education as an artist."[120]

Raphael's obvious desire to retaliate against a detractor—even if it meant adding a few years to his training (which lasted for five years, instead of eight)—is understandable. But for the AAM, it was a successful campaign to redirect public attention from its own shortcomings and discredit an important rival in arts education in Montreal. This attack marked a turning point in William Raphael's career. If he persisted in giving courses, he realized that it would no longer be possible for him to reconnect with this network. His new works were increasingly ignored by the critics; all eyes were now on Brymner and his entourage.

Compared to Raphael, who had been active in Montreal cultural circles for nearly thirty years, Brymner was a relative newcomer. But he could boast of his recent training in Paris, notably at the Académie Julian, with teachers such as William Bouguereau (1825–1905).[121] Both his training and his work—with its focus on a lighter palette and bucolic subjects—appealed to the bourgeois tastes of the time. Brymner soon marked Canadian art with these aesthetic trends, which also contributed to changes in people's appraisal of Raphael's work (fig. 52–53). As a man of the clan,[122] Brymner didn't hesitate to exclude Raphael from his orbit, and then, on the strength of his authority and his position at the AAM, he began to question Raphael's teaching in public lectures.[123]

In 1890, Raphael helped found a new cultural association, the Pen and Pencil Club, but he had to distance himself from it when Brymner and Harris became members the following year.[124] Raphael also resigned from the Royal Canadian Academy of Arts in 1896, no doubt disheartened by the institution's lack of financial support for his career and the reality of the professional and social landscape of Montreal.[125]

Later Years

By the end of the nineteenth century, William Raphael had a large family of children and grandchildren. Some of them settled in the United States, while his youngest daughter and her father-in-law lived in his home. He continued his work but kept his distance from the power struggles he'd experienced for so many years. He revisited some favourite subjects in his repertoire, creating peaceful landscapes, such as *Two Women in Rowboat Near Shoreline*, July 5, 1911 (fig. 54), and scenes from everyday life, such as *The Artist's House in Victoria St.*, 1908 (fig. 55), as well as portraits of his family and even his beloved dogs (fig. 56).

Still active as a teacher, Raphael told a journalist in 1888 that "[w]ithout teaching, no local artist could live here."[126] His studio welcomed students until around 1909, and in 1896, he also agreed to teach art classes in Sherbrooke, in the Art Building erected in 1887.[127] Until his last days, he remained available to give lessons and advice to the

Fig 57 Sister Marie-Hélène-de-la-Croix, *Portrait of William Raphael*, c.1911, oil on canvas, 33 x 18 cm, Musée de Lachine, Montreal. **Fig 58** William Raphael, *Where I Was Born—Nakel, Prussia*, n.d., oil on panel, 26.7 x 19.7 cm, collection of Jonathan Wener, Montreal.

religious community of the Sisters of Sainte-Anne.[128] Over the years, he had met and trained several nuns, including Sister Marie-Hélène-de-la-Croix (née Élisabeth Martin, 1861–1956). For their part, the nuns had repeatedly demonstrated their appreciation of his knowledge and pedagogy. In 1910, the community acquired Raphael's collection of plasters. In a letter dated September 17, he wrote: "I am most pleased to know that my Collection will be in an institution in which I had the pleasure to be for many years so well acquainted with many of the Sisters."[129]

Sister Marie-Hélène-de-la-Croix and the entire community of nuns were quick to recognize the qualities of both artist and teacher. In 1911, Sister Marie-Hélène painted a portrait of Raphael, which she presented to him as a gift in 1912.[130] At the same time, she was probably working on a second portrait, to be kept in the congregation's painting studio (fig. 57). She took pains to keep the format and dimensions consistent with a series of previously purchased works representing the great painters of the Renaissance and Baroque periods. The portrait of William Raphael eventually became part of a suite of paintings of artists including Leonardo da Vinci (1452–1519), Raphael, Titian (c.1488–1576), Peter Paul Rubens (1577–1640), Anthony van Dyck (1599–1641), and Guido Reni (1575–1642). In this way, the Montreal painter took his place among the great masters of art history.

At the beginning of the twentieth century, Raphael no longer enjoyed the prestige he had in the late 1870s. His works were not the talk of the newspapers. Although a few people still came to chat with the old artist in his studio (fig. 59), he didn't seek the attention of the art world. His professional and personal work was done, and he could look back in peace on the full life he had lived, from Nakel (fig. 58) to Montreal. When he died on March 13, 1914, the last tributes to the painter appeared in the daily papers.[131] Despite his disconnection from the cultural scene in the twilight of his life, the artist was not entirely forgotten.

Fig 59 William Raphael in his studio, c.1905, photographer unknown, collection of Jonathan Wener, Montreal.

Key Works

Fig 60 William Raphael, *Haymarket Square / Victoria Square*, 1861, oil on canvas, 51.1 x 63.5 cm, collection of Jonathan Wener, Montreal.

Haymarket Square / Victoria Square, 1861

Painted at the beginning of William Raphael's career, this work is an example of his talent for depicting nineteenth-century urban life (fig. 60). With this piece, Raphael showcases his ability to create a genre scene that takes up the principles of the Biedermeier movement, which favoured realistic portrayals of everyday life. Here, he captures the bustle of the Montreal haymarket in Victoria Square.[1]

The square was named in honour of Queen Victoria (1819–1901) following the October 1860 royal visit of her son, the future Edward VII (1841–1910).[2] This trading space was an essential part of the city and provided a connection to the surrounding farms and lands. Locals went to the square to buy supplies for their horses and cattle, which at the time played a crucial role in transporting goods and people.

An 1866 photograph of Victoria Square produced by the William Notman Studio shows that Raphael strove for accuracy in his work (fig. 61). The painting is also comparable to a scene created by James Duncan (1806–1881) in 1853, the same year as a series of riots that broke out in front of the Zion Church in response to anti-Catholic speeches given by Alessandro Gavazzi, an Italian religious reformer (fig. 62). While Raphael and Duncan are both exacting in their depictions of the space, they frame it in very different ways: Duncan takes a more panoramic view, while Raphael invites us into the square, closer to its activity.

In the right foreground of Raphael's painting, we see a wood sawyer and a water vendor, representing the various small trades associated with this Montreal landmark. In the centre, a barefoot child drinks from the "fountain of health," a stone structure crowned with an image of a beaver.[3] A harnessed horse also drinks from the fountain, while its owner stands patiently on his empty cart. To the left, a full load of hay is pulled by a white horse escorted by a man who threatens the animal with his whip. These two carts, full and empty, underline the idea of exchanges taking place in the market space. Further on, in the middle ground, several carriages are grouped together. One of the carts, heavily laden, passes through the central opening of a symmetrical red-brick building. This is a weighing building, constructed in 1842; it's essential for determining the weight and value of any hay load.[4]

Raphael also offers, in great detail, a precise view of the buildings that surrounded the square at the time. To the far left, part of the facade of St. Andrew's, a Presbyterian church destroyed by fire in 1869, is visible. More centrally, a sloping roof, its peak decorated with a cross, can be seen. This is the Unitarian Church of the Messiah (destroyed by fire in 1987), whose front face is marked by arched stained-glass windows. On the right-hand side of the composition, recognizable by its grey roof and dormer windows, is the Hospice Sainte-Brigide (demolished in 1900), a shelter for the sick, the destitute, and the homeless.

Fig 61 (ABOVE) William Notman Studio, *Beaver Hall Hill from Victoria Square, Montreal, QC, 1866*, 1866, silver salts on paper mounted on paper, albumen process, 8.5 x 5.6 cm, McCord Stewart Museum, Montreal. **Fig 62** (BELOW) James Duncan, *The Gavazzi Riot in Montreal*, 1853, watercolour, sepia ink, graphite, and gouache on wove paper, 32.6 x 41.3 cm, Museum of Civilization, Quebec City.

Behind Bonsecours Market, Montreal, 1866

This painting (fig. 63), produced in 1866, is a central work in William Raphael's oeuvre because of both its larger format and the critical attention it received. It seems to spontaneously capture a bustling city street, with crowds gathering near the temporary stalls that line the Bonsecours Market, a landmark of Montreal's old port. Although it has a snapshot-like quality, the work was actually the fruit of several years of effort, with Raphael producing numerous versions that provoked a variety of responses from art critics of his era. This significant composition—exemplary of Raphael's masterful application of Biedermeier principles—has endured: it was selected for the cover of the first edition of *The Illustrated History of Canada* in 1987.

Two drawings by Raphael reveal the beginnings of *Behind Bonsecours Market*. Around 1857, he drew a violin player (fig. 64) and an architectural view of the rear of the Notre-Dame-de-Bon-Secours Chapel: two motifs that he repeated years later. But it was only in 1865 that he produced his first painting depicting the back of the famous market. Small in scale, that piece was presented in September of that year at the Montreal Provincial Exhibition. Included in the fine arts section of the event, held at the Crystal Palace, the work attracted the lukewarm attention of an anonymous correspondent from the *Journal de Québec*.[1] The reporter began by criticizing the artist's name—"It's such a difficult name for a painter to bear that it's ridiculous"—and then he went on to write a mixed review of the piece: "[T]he scene this artist treats is quite skilfully rendered: it's the Bonsecours market on the banks of the river. The group of peasants is well done, but some of the characters, especially the listeners to the strolling fiddler, verge on caricature, and that's a fault."[2]

A second critical review appeared in the newspaper *La Minerve*. Once again anonymous, this appraisal complained more about the subject matter than the composition: "But why, in all the *Bonsecours markets* (of which there are many) signed by Raphaël, Duncan or others, are Canadians always given outfits and expressions that would be impossible to notice in their habits today?"[3]

The two reviews, both published on September 27, 1865, could have been by the same hand, and might even have been penned by Napoléon Bourassa (1827–1916), an artist renowned for his writings on and knowledge of the Renaissance masters, including Fra Angelico (1395–1455) and Raphael (1483–1520).[4] Some months earlier, in an issue of *La Revue canadienne*, Bourassa had critiqued a William Raphael painting exhibited the previous year at the salon of the Art Association of Montreal. That painting, depicting a street scene in front of the Bonsecours Market, had earned these mocking words: "We do have a Raphaël, who last year painted our Bonsecours Market, with lots of sheep, calves, cows, pigs, broods… under the effect of a setting sun; but we must confess with humility, this Raphaël is not the right one—I hope I can say this without insulting him."[5] Making no secret of his displeasure with the artist's name and the caricatured appearance of some of his figures, Bourassa wrote in a way that seems too similar to the texts published in September 1865 to be ignored.

William Raphael was aware of the pejorative comments about his skills. These remarks seemed to him all the more inappropriate when his work won first prize for oil painting at the exhibition.[6] In response to the insults, Raphael produced a variation of his piece the following year. In that version, he incorporated a deliberately caricatured figure of a blind critic who stands in the way of foreign artists wishing to enter Montreal.[7] The work was sent to Scotland in November 1866 and probably purchased at its exhibition.[8] To date, it has not been traced.

In February 1867, Raphael displayed a new larger version of *Behind Bonsecours Market* at the Art Association of Montreal exhibition.[9] This was most likely the work now in the collection of the National Gallery of Canada, and it was an ambitious piece for an artist still at the beginning of his career. The composition is marked by a large diagonal that runs down the roofs and across the painting to the lower right. In this way, the canvas is separated between the vast sky and luminous blue of the water and the bustle of people crowding around the market.

The work is dynamic and also sonorous, even noisy. An elderly man listens to the music of a fiddler, his hand resting on an axe (fig. 66). Two children, one of them a little blonde girl who pensively places the index finger of her left hand on her mouth, watch the musician attentively. To the sounds of the violin is added the murmur of the many conversations taking place. Some people on the left seem to be negotiating the price of various commodities, while those in the centre are chatting, having perhaps unexpectedly crossed paths as they went about their business. On the slope behind them, the sound of horses and the creaking of carts can be heard.

Inspired by life in Montreal, Raphael thus offers his view of activities carried out by modest people of diverse origins with whom he can even identify. In fact, some experts believe that the figure in the centre, carrying a portfolio and a candlestick, is a self-portrait (fig. 65).[10]

Fig 63 William Raphael, *Behind Bonsecours Market, Montreal*, 1866, oil on canvas, 67.5 x 109.6 cm, National Gallery of Canada, Ottawa.

Fig 64 William Raphael, *Man Playing Violin Under Lamppost*, 1857, graphite on wove paper, 20.1 x 11.6 cm, National Gallery of Canada, Ottawa.

Fig 65 William Raphael, *Behind Bonsecours Market, Montreal* (detail), 1866, oil on canvas, 67.5 x 109.6 cm, National Gallery of Canada, Ottawa.

Fig 66 William Raphael, *Behind Bonsecours Market, Montreal* (detail), 1866, oil on canvas, 67.5 x 109.6 cm, National Gallery of Canada, Ottawa.

Fig 67 Roberts & Reinhold, after William Raphael, *The Early Bird Picks Up the Worm*, 1869, chromolithograph, Library and Archives Canada, Ottawa.

The Early Bird Picks Up the Worm, 1869

The Early Bird Picks Up the Worm was painted by William Raphael in 1868 and reproduced as a chromolithograph, or full-colour print, the following year (fig. 67). Lighthearted but with an element of morality, the work draws on the well-known proverb about the early bird getting the worm. It is noteworthy not just as a reflection of the artist's sense of humour but as a reminder of the interest in chromolithographic reproduction in Canada in the 1860s.

This painting appears to be a reworking of a similar piece by Raphael called *The Rival Beggars*, 1861 (fig. 68). While he retained the composition of the earlier work, he altered the appearance of the man on the left, the shape of the door separating the figures, and the overall architectural context to make the dome of the Bonsecours Market visible in the distance. The tone of the piece has changed as well. In the reworked version, the man on the left wears a satisfied expression as he emerges from a house with a bag filled with food. The other man, also in search of food, cannot hide his disappointment as he realizes he's arrived too late and the charity of the homeowners has likely already been exhausted.[1]

In March 1869, Roberts & Reinhold, a high-quality Montreal printing studio, produced a chromolithograph of *The Early Bird Picks Up the Worm*. The work was immediately heralded in the press as a technical breakthrough surpassing all previous attempts in the field.[2] The newspaper *Le Pays* was particularly effusive in its praise. "The artist, Mr. Reinhold, has given his painting all the vigour and depth of oil painting," the paper reported. "Lovers of the fine arts among us should take pride in encouraging as much as possible this new art, which brings the productions of the great masters within everyone's reach, and tends to popularize the love of beauty."[3]

At a price of just three dollars apiece, chromolithographs were affordable and made it possible for "many Canadian homes… to boast of oil-paintings which never did so before," according to the *Daily Witness*.[4] Collectors, artists, and critics alike saw the value in reproducing works in full colour with great accuracy. Among lithographers, Roberts & Reinhold stood out for their technical ingenuity and the quality of their creations. After becoming business partners in 1864, Rudolf Reinhold and William Roberts presented their work at many provincial exhibitions and won some awards.[5]

While chromolithography ensured a democratization of art, the process was complex and required specialized know-how. The chromolithograph of *The Early Bird Picks Up the Worm*, for example, needed twenty-one progressive proofs, with each one adding colour to the image until it was complete.[6] Two full sets of these proofs have been preserved at the National Gallery of Canada and the Château Ramezay museum in Montreal. They provide a better understanding of the chromolithographic technique and constitute an exceptional case study of how colour prints were made in Canada during the nineteenth century.[7] Generally, such series, which detail the stages in the reproduction process, have not been preserved, making these proofs particularly noteworthy in the history of Canadian art.

Fig 68 William Raphael, *The Rival Beggars*, 1861, oil on canvas, 66 x 61 cm, collection of Jonathan Wener, Montreal.

Fig 69 William Raphael, *Tandem*, 1869, oil on canvas, 56.5 x 92.3 cm, Musée national des beaux-arts du Québec, Quebec City.

Tandem, 1869

With its diagonal composition, *Tandem* is a dynamic painting that highlights the reality of the Canadian winter, with the darkness on the horizon portending a snowstorm (fig. 69). The work was immediately presented to the public by gallery owner William Scott, who must have been delighted to discover this new piece by an esteemed painter. It was praised in the January 29 edition of the *Evening Star*, which noted that the "peltering and indefinite [*sic*] storm of snow and hail… is very characteristic of our winter."[1]

Although it was not unusual to see sleighs represented in Canadian art—they appear in works by artists from James Peachey (d.1797) to Cornelius Krieghoff (1815–1872) (fig. 70)—the painting, with its depiction of children and a winter storm, reflects Raphael's interest in themes that had been relatively unexplored at the time. Art historian Mario Béland's description of the work could not be more accurate:

> [A] boy, in a hurry to avoid the storm, drives a sled loaded with firewood and pulled by two dogs. On either side of the sled, two other boys keep the beasts moving with their shouts, sticks or whips. Farther back, standing out against the dark mass of clouds, a woman sunken in the snow, probably the mother, painstakingly follows the group with the youngest child. To the left, at the bottom of a hill, the typical Canadian log cabin![2]

Despite the threat of the coming snow, the work exudes joyfulness. The children, no doubt pleased with the speed of their sled, make funny faces. The one on the left even smiles broadly as he shows the young driver how to place his hands to control the steering. Even the work's title, *Tandem*, was chosen to amuse the viewer: at the time, the word "tandem" was used to describe luxurious sleighs pulled by two horses, harnessed one in front of the other. Raphael's depiction of these young people, whose makeshift sleigh is simply pulled by two dogs, is also a sly nod to the prestigious Tandem Clubs of Montreal and Quebec City, whose excursions were elaborate parades to show off their members' wealth and refinement (fig. 71).[3]

In a sign of its success, the 1869 composition was repeated in another version in 1878 (fig. 142), with more emphasis placed on the young boys, who have managed to turn the winter chore of fetching firewood into a game.[4] The mother, seen in the earlier piece trudging through the snow with her youngest child in tow, has disappeared, and the blackened sky heralding the storm now gives a slight glimpse of clearing.

Fig 70 (ABOVE) Cornelius Krieghoff, *Montmorency Falls*, 1853, oil on canvas, 91.4 x 121.9 cm, Art Gallery of Ontario, Toronto.
Fig 71 (BELOW) James Duncan, *The Quebec Tandem Club, Champ De Mars, Montreal*, c.1840, watercolour and gouache over soft pencil on paper, 32.2 x 47.0 cm, Royal Ontario Museum, Toronto.

Fig 72 William Raphael, *Tandem* (detail), 1869, oil on canvas, 56.5 x 92.3 cm, Musée national des beaux-arts du Québec, Quebec City.

Fig 73 William Raphael, *Tandem* (detail), 1869, oil on canvas, 56.5 x 92.3 cm, Musée national des beaux-arts du Québec, Quebec City.

Fig 74 William Raphael, after James Inglis, *The McFarlane Children*, 1871, oil on canvas, mounted on Masonite, 114.8 x 90.5 x 0.4 cm, National Gallery of Canada, Ottawa.

The McFarlane Children, 1871

In the years following his arrival in Montreal in 1857, William Raphael produced numerous portraits of prominent members of Canadian society. The painting *The McFarlane Children* (fig. 74), although made later, is nonetheless part of this early practice. This work, which is also an example of a group portrait of children from the same family, is reminiscent of the portraits of children painted by Théophile Hamel (1817–1870) in the middle of the century[1] and the photographic portraits produced by William Notman (1826–1891). These works reveal a new sentimentality—one tinged with affection—for childhood during the Victorian period.

This piece, which is part photograph and part painting, also demonstrates Raphael's use of photography as a resource for his work. Since its invention in the 1830s, photography has been regarded as a documentary tool as much as an art form. But it nonetheless quickly slipped into the sphere of activity of painters, creating important connections between the disciplines. While some abandoned their brushes and became photographers, others collaborated with photography studios, even using photographic images to compose their paintings.

William Raphael put his talents to work for William Notman and Abner Bedee Taber (1832–1866), thus developing relationships with two of the most important Canadian photographers of the day. *The McFarlane Children* is a rare example of the collaboration between Raphael and photographer James Inglis (1835–1904).[2] The portrait is signed in the lower left-hand corner of the composition, first with the inscription "J. Inglis Photo" and then, below that, with "W. Raphael fecit." *Fecit* is a Latin word meaning "did"—or in this case, "painted." The names of the two men are followed by the date of creation, 1871.

This work, now in the collection of the National Gallery of Canada, was commissioned by David McFarlane.[3] Born in Glasgow, McFarlane settled in Montreal in 1854. Although he was not part of the financial elite, he managed to establish himself in a favourable middle-class position, working for Alex Buntin & Co., a firm that sold office supplies and paper. In 1857, he married Margaret Kennedy and started a family, which by 1871 included five children: Margaret, David Jr., Jean, Ann, and Clement Hugh. Caught up in the Victorian era vogue for photographic portraits, the McFarlanes called on another new Canadian from Scotland, James Inglis, to immortalize their offspring.

Renowned for his composite portraits, Inglis devised the triangular composition of the 1871 work, with young Clement Hugh on a three-wheeled varnished wooden baby carriage in the foreground. Inglis precisely determined the position and posture to be adopted by each of the children, and then set about printing individual portraits of them—notably the *Portrait of Jeanie McFarlane* and the *Portrait of Annie McFarlane* (fig. 75–76). With composite photography, the photographs are printed on paper and then the figures are cut out following their contours, assembled, and pasted onto a painted backdrop, usually of an atmospheric landscape. The collage is then harmonized by retouching and integrating the figures into the backdrop. Finally, the collage is photographed so it can be printed in various copies. In this particular case, Inglis called on Raphael to paint a photographic enlargement of the composition instead of limiting himself to black-and-white prints alone.

Raphael, who had already done this type of work for Notman and Taber at the start of his Montreal career, carried out the commission by reworking the entire surface. He added more saturated colours to the dresses, ribbons, and stroller. Notably, he also paid attention to the colour of the trees, whose foliage is brushed more broadly to produce the blurred effect of the background. Finally, the faces are meticulously painted using an interplay of thin, transparent coats of paint and polished strokes, to respect the photographic likeness.

Fig 75 (LEFT) James Inglis, *Portrait of Jeanie McFarlane*, 1871, National Gallery of Canada, Ottawa. **Fig 76** (RIGHT) James Inglis, *Portrait of Annie McFarlane*, 1871, National Gallery of Canada, Ottawa.

Fig 77 William Raphael, after James Inglis, *The McFarlane Children* (detail), 1871, oil on canvas, mounted on Masonite, 114.8 x 90.5 x 0.4 cm, National Gallery of Canada, Ottawa.

Fig 78 William Raphael, after James Inglis, *The McFarlane Children* (detail), 1871, oil on canvas, mounted on Masonite, 114.8 x 90.5 x 0.4 cm, National Gallery of Canada, Ottawa.

Fig 79 William Raphael, *Habitant* (or *Preparing to Smoke*), c.1872–1910, oil on canvas, 35 x 27 cm, collection of Jonathan Wener, Montreal.

Habitant (or *Preparing to Smoke*), c.1872–1910

In the early 1870s, William Raphael introduced an approach that would later become a recurrent part of his work. In a departure from the genre scenes and portraits that had defined so much of his practice, he began to paint highly simplified renderings of French Canadian habitants—generally farmers living in rural Quebec—shown in domestic settings (fig. 79). The image seen here is somewhat indebted to Cornelius Krieghoff (1815–1872) and his *Le Fumeur*, c.1855–1860 (fig. 80), and precedes by several years the work of Marc-Aurèle de Foy Suzor-Coté (1869–1937), who often painted the same subject, as in *Le Père Moreau*, 1921 (fig. 81). For Raphael, this new approach allowed him to reconstruct, in a sensitive and empathetic way, the world of these modest people.

The first known example of this subject in Raphael's work is found in a lithograph produced in 1872 (fig. 82). The figure is identified as "Mr. Sarrasin" from Saint-Gabriel-de-Brandon.[1] Later, Raphael stopped naming the model in order to give a more encompassing scope to his depictions of rural French Canadian life. He produced variations and replicas of the subject until the end of his career.

The bearded man in *Habitant* (or *Preparing to Smoke*), painted between 1872 and 1910, is shown in a rustic setting, his face in profile, holding a pipe in his hands. There are no protruding red noses or toothless mouths, as in some of Krieghoff's paintings, to provoke humour; Raphael's habitant is portrayed in a solemn—even pensive—attitude. He is dressed in traditional winter garb: a hood fastened with a long red sash, a blue tuque, and moccasins. He's seated on a simple wooden chair; on the floor is a dark brown spittoon, for chewing tobacco, on a pink catalogne (or woven carpet) with burgundy-red, straw-yellow, green, and pale-pink stripes.[2] Next to the man is a large double-decker wood stove decorated with reliefs.[3] Massive and low, it also features a round opening at the bottom (for adjusting the air draft), allowing a glimpse of the bright fire within. On top are a kettle and a metal saucepan. The latter, despite its lid, lets out a few clouds of steam. The decor is limited to a wall shelf on the left and a narrow hanging sheet on the right. The man is motionless; the artist has focused on his clothes and surroundings.

This type of work (fig. 37, 83, 126), although sober, was very popular with collectors of the period.[4] In 1880, for example, the Marquess of Lorne (1845–1914), then governor general of Canada, purchased one of Raphael's paintings of a habitant.[5] In 1882, that composition was made into an engraving by C.J. Wardell and inserted in the book *Picturesque Canada*, as the frontispiece to the chapter entitled "French-Canadian Life and Character."[6] By appearing in this important work, the image thus becomes the emblematic figure of French-speaking Quebec. The habitant, as described by the book's author, George Monro Grant, is a farmer attached to conservative, traditional values and a "hard worker" smoking "the evil-smelling native tobacco."[7]

Fig 80 (LEFT) Cornelius Krieghoff, *The Smoker* (*Le Fumeur*), c.1855–60, oil on canvas, 28.8 x 26.3 cm, Musée national des beaux-arts du Québec, Quebec City. **Fig 81** (RIGHT) Marc-Aurèle de Foy Suzor-Coté, *Father Moreau* (*Le Père Moreau*), 1921, charcoal on paper glued to cardboard, 41.4 x 30.1 cm, Musée national des beaux-arts du Québec, Quebec City.

Fig 82 William Raphael, *Mr. Sarrasin, St. Gabriel de Brandon (holding pipe)*, 1872, lithograph, 23.8 x 16.5 cm, collection of Jonathan Wener, Montreal.

Fig 83 William Raphael, *Habitant at Home*, 1873, oil on paper laid down on cardboard, 26.1 x 19.7 cm, collection of Jonathan Wener, Montreal.

Fig 84 William Raphael, *Indian Encampment on the Lower St. Lawrence Estuary*, 1879, oil on canvas, 61.3 x 107 cm, National Gallery of Canada, Ottawa.

Indian Encampment on the Lower St. Lawrence Estuary, 1879

In the winter of 1879, William Raphael painted a landscape of the Charlevoix region showing the impressive Cap-Blanc cliff at Murray Bay (La Malbaie) and the St. Lawrence River, all under a moonlit sky (fig. 84). The work admirably displays Raphael's mastery of landscape painting, which is perhaps what prompted him to submit it as his reception piece in 1880 to the newly founded Canadian Academy of Arts (renamed the Royal Canadian Academy of Arts in 1882).

This dark, mysterious landscape is a fine demonstration of the artist's understanding of various light sources. The fire in one of the tepees illuminates the scene with a few reddish flashes and attracts the viewer's attention. In the distance, the faint beam from a lighthouse shines out to sea. The St. Lawrence flows through the right-hand side of the painting, overhung by heavy clouds whose contours are illuminated by the moon. Its silvery light also manages to pierce a gap to reach the waves below. For this composition, Raphael drew on sketches he had made on location the previous summer (fig. 87), as well as on a number of earlier paintings, such as *Encampment by the River*, 1871 (fig. 88), which also depicted an Indigenous people's camp.

Raphael exhibited *Indian Encampment on the Lower St. Lawrence Estuary* at the seventh annual exhibition of the Ontario Society of Artists in May 1879. The *Globe* newspaper described it as the artist's most successful work at the event.[1] Then, in March 1880, the painting was displayed at the first exhibition of the Canadian Academy of Arts, held at Ottawa's Clarendon Hotel, and subsequently submitted to the institution, completing Raphael's bid to obtain full membership.[2] The painting thus became one of the first pieces in the Canadian national collection (soon to form the core of the National Gallery of Canada collection). Given the academy's preference for landscapes, it was no accident that Raphael opted for this painting of a dramatic night scene.[3] The work is tinged with a late Romanticism that is uncommon in the artist's output but that animated the works of many of his contemporaries.

But the painting was not universally admired. In the March 20 issue of the satirical newspaper *Grip*, it was included in a set entitled "Diploma Pictures—Presented to the New National Gallery," which caricatured the reception pieces submitted to the academy (fig. 85). Raphael's composition is reduced to a pile of tepees invading the entire surface of the work. Contrary to the caricaturist's vision, the Indigenous encampment is far less prominent in the original image: the dark silhouette of Cap-Blanc set against the blue sky attracts much more attention, as do the reflections of moonlight. Raphael also departs from the stereotypical cartoonish idea of tepees and takes care to offer a realistic representation of Indigenous dwellings, including a squat-looking hut built of bark and wood. With its sloping roof, this hut corresponds in every respect to the dwellings photographed on the site by the Livernois studio around 1873 (fig. 86).

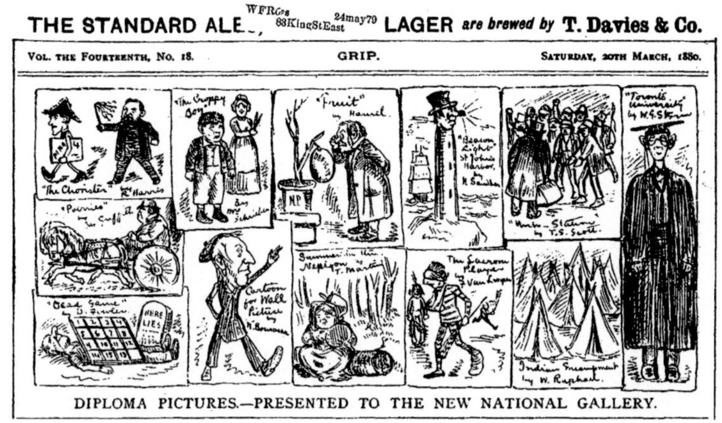

Fig 85 (ABOVE) Artist unknown, *Diploma Pictures—Presented to the New National Gallery*, 1880, caricature published in *Grip* 14, no. 18 (March 20, 1880). **Fig 86** (BELOW) Livernois Studio, *Aboriginal Bark Huts and Basket Maker, Murray Bay, QC*, c.1873, albumen process, 15.3 x 20.3 cm, McCord Stewart Museum, Montreal.

Fig 87 William Raphael, *Murray Bay*, July 30, 1878, graphite on wove paper, 9.4 x 14.6 cm, National Gallery of Canada, Ottawa.

Fig 88 William Raphael, *Encampment by the River*, 1871, oil on canvas, 27.9 x 41.9 cm, private collection.

Dr. Roddick's Remarkable Case of Favus, Showing the Distribution of the Scabs and the Extent of the Eruption on the Body, 1880

During the 1870s and 1880s, William Raphael received various commissions from a young physician named William Osler, who had become a professor at McGill University in 1875 and would go on to be one of the most important figures in Canadian medical history.[1] These commissions—drawings of pathologies intended to illustrate the doctor's research and writings—were nothing like Raphael's usual subjects. *Dr. Roddick's Remarkable Case of Favus, Showing the Distribution of the Scabs and the Extent of the Eruption on the Body* (fig. 91) exemplifies his rigour in anatomical representation.

To create these images, Raphael relied as much on a long artistic tradition of anatomical study as he did the collaboration of medical experts.[2] Indeed, during his training in Berlin, he had already acquired detailed knowledge of the human body. The academic approach required students to draw the particularities of the flesh, as well as meticulously examine the body's interior organs and structures (fig. 89). It was even customary to draw skinned cadavers so as to be able to recognize the various muscles and better capture their details.[3]

These journeys into medical illustration were also reflected in sketches from Raphael's student years, when he sometimes drew fragments of flayed bodies. When Osler called upon his talents, Raphael was probably not entirely taken aback by the types of images the doctor wanted. Although the commission was far removed from the quest for beauty that preoccupies many artists, and contact with death and disease can obviously trouble anyone, Raphael proved to be skilled at anatomical draughtsmanship. He was careful to spare no detail, while taking the most objective, dispassionate approach possible.

Osler's appreciation of Raphael's work was so great that the doctor even called on the artist from abroad. In 1884, Osler became a professor of medicine at the University of Pennsylvania and began to entrust Raphael with tasks from a distance, noting in one letter that "there is nobody here who can do such fine anatomical work."[4]

Raphael's commissions for Dr. Osler included three plates that appeared in the book *Montreal General Hospital: Reports Clinical and Pathological*, published in 1880 by Dawson Brothers, a well-known local firm. In this book, edited by Osler, Raphael's work was reproduced by John Henry Walker (1831–1899), an engraver renowned for his preference for xylography (woodcut printing) and his numerous contributions to Montreal newspapers.[5] Plate III features two figures illustrating "Atresia of pulmonary artery, with patent Ductus Arteriosus" and "Ductus Arteriosus and Arch of Aorta in case of General Dropsy of Foetus." Plate VII features two figures associated with "Dr. Roddick's Case of Occipital Meningocele" (fig. 90). And plate VIII shows a child suffering from an infectious skin disease called favus, a type of ringworm (fig. 91).

The posture of the child, who is seen naked and from the side, reveals the extent of the disease eating away at his skin. At the same time, the pose, with legs apart and left arm raised, is reminiscent of that expected of live models during workshop sessions. Indeed, it was common practice at the time to simulate body movements during poses as depicted in a drawing by Raphael created in Berlin, *Boy Standing in Profile*, 1854.[6] The result is a singular image that, for all its interest, did not find a home in Raphael's painted work; rather, it rested within the pages of Osler's book, to be seen only by those eager to develop their medical knowledge.

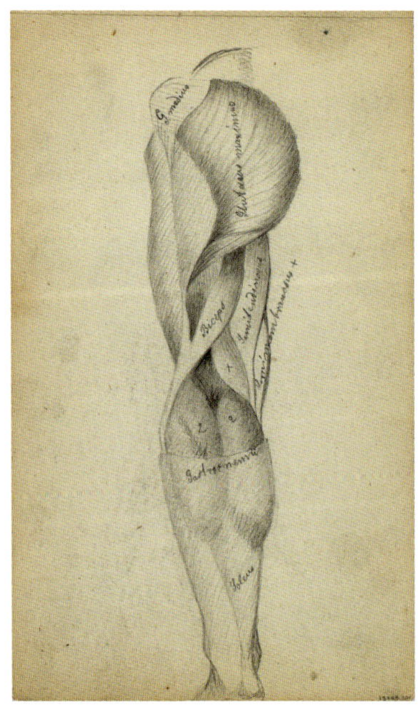

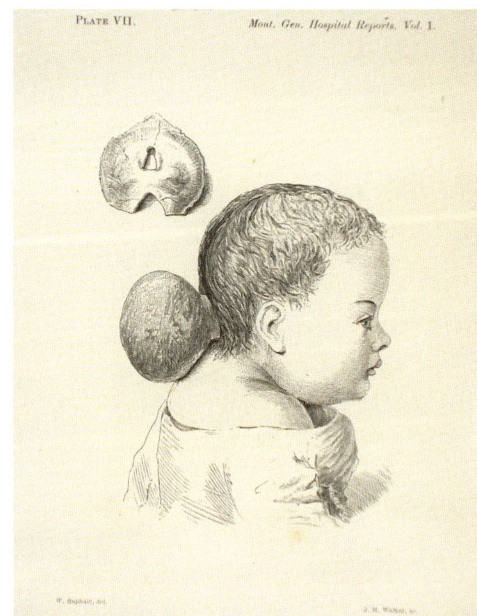

Fig 89 (LEFT) William Raphael, *Anatomy Study of Leg Muscles*, 1853–57, graphite on wove paper, 16.8 x 10.5 cm, National Gallery of Canada, Ottawa. **Fig 90** (RIGHT) John Henry Walker, after William Raphael, *Dr. Roddick's Case of Occipital Meningocele*, 1880, ink on paper, 23.9 x 14.2 cm, McCord Stewart Museum, Montreal.

Fig 91 John Henry Walker, after William Raphael, *Dr. Roddick's Remarkable Case of Favus, Showing the Distribution of the Scabs and the Extent of the Eruption on the Body*, 1880, ink on paper, 23.9 x 14 cm, McCord Stewart Museum, Montreal.

Fig 92 William Raphael, *Sawmill and Hydraulic Dam*, 1889, oil on canvas, 30.5 x 40.6 cm, collection of Jonathan Wener, Montreal.

Sawmill and Hydraulic Dam, 1889

William Raphael was not blind to the changes wrought by humans on the world around them. In his landscapes, the painter, a lover of the outdoors, explored themes closely associated with the exploitation of natural resources. Locks, dams, and mines were often present in his paintings from this time, as seen in *Sawmill and Hydraulic Dam* from 1889 (fig. 92). This piece captures not only the industrial development of the province but also its growing appeal to tourists. Cruises were becoming increasingly popular in Quebec, making it possible for visitors to discover the sawmills on the Saint-Maurice and Saguenay Rivers. Industry and tourism became linked as more people explored the landscapes of the province.[1]

With *Sawmill and Hydraulic Dam*, Raphael captured a fresh and realistic scene. Planks of wood pile up below the mill, while in the foreground, three logs have been spared. Torrents of water pour out of the dam next to the grey mill, with the white eddies giving way to clear water that breaks against a few rocks in the current. In the background, two other grey buildings blend into the landscape between lush green trees.

The painting's strong sketchy character—reminiscent of smaller works on cardboard, such as *Dam on the St. Charles River*, August 11, 1874 (fig. 93)—reveals Raphael's speed of execution. Working in situ, he used very diluted paint to render the bank in the foreground. He then drew several lines to highlight the rectangular shape of the planks, the fineness of which contrasts with the highly textured sky, which was probably executed with a knife. The grain of the canvas can be seen in the texture of the clouds, and the entire surface is marked by the artist's omnipresent brushstrokes, which are particularly pronounced in the trees.

This work may have led to a larger finished painting produced in the studio, as suggested by two pieces exhibited at salons in the following years. In 1891, Raphael presented a work entitled *The Mill* at a Royal Canadian Academy of Arts salon held in Toronto.[2] And three years later, the Art Association of Montreal exhibited a work called *The Mill Dam*, whose "details are carefully manipulated,"[3] according to the critic of the *Daily Witness* newspaper. Although these last two paintings cannot be located at present, they are a reminder that the subject sketched in 1889 deserved, in the artist's opinion, to be developed further.

Fig 93 William Raphael, *Dam on the St. Charles River*, August 11, 1874, oil on cardboard, 36 x 29.4 cm, Musée de Lachine, Montreal.

Fig 94 William Raphael, *With the Current*, 1892, oil on canvas, 40.8 x 63.5 cm, Montreal Museum of Fine Arts.

With the Current, 1892

With the Current (fig. 94) reflects William Raphael's love of the outdoors—a passion he pursued throughout his career. Floating gently on the waves, two people revel in the sunshine and the tranquillity of a red canoe. They sit back to back, the woman fly fishing while the man, cigarette in mouth, reads his newspaper. Their posture and the colour of their clothes—one in white sitting upright, the other in black and semi-reclined—provide contrast, as do the woman's elegant hat and the man's simple yarmulke, a reference to his Jewish heritage. The bright red of the boat also stands out against the verdant landscape. These differences are echoed in the artist's pictorial approach: the canvas shows a range of brushstrokes, from the most sustained academic technique in the treatment of the two figures to the heavy, visible brushstrokes that build up the background. Despite these dissimilarities, the work as a whole is harmonious. The peaceful, even intimate scene is set against a natural backdrop, with the expanse of dark water in the foreground doubling the couple's image in a stunningly rendered reflection.

Raphael travelled extensively in the summer months. He came back from each trip with several drawings in his sketchbooks and many pochades (quick sketches), which would later prove invaluable in his work. During the summers of 1891 and 1892, the artist visited Richmond and Otterburn Park, both in Quebec, as well as Long Island and Norfolk in the United States. Along the way, he collected details of trees and water features—all motifs that could be put to good use in future paintings produced in his studio.

Before he painted *With the Current*, Raphael had already tackled the subject of people on a canoe trip several times, including in *The Boating Party*, 1876 (fig. 95), and in a sketch made at Sainte-Rose in 1884. In these works, however, the figures are merely details intended to enhance the landscape by amplifying its scale. In *With the Current*, Raphael reversed the formula: nature lost its primacy and became a setting for the true subjects of the work, a man and woman captured in a moment of serenity. Drawing on landscapes he had visited many times, Raphael creates an intimate composition, closing off the background with dense, dark vegetation. In this way, he manages not only to focus attention on the duo but also to cut them off from the world, leaving them alone in this suspended moment.

Apparently pleased with this work, Raphael produced a variant, *Throwing the Bait, River St. Charles, Quebec*, in 1895 (fig. 96). In this later version, the mountains in the background are bathed in a bluish light. The couple, alone in their own world, are a poignant metaphor for Raphael's late-career period, when he withdrew from the art world in search of calmness in both his life and his subjects.

Fig 95 (ABOVE) William Raphael, *The Boating Party*, 1876, oil on canvas, 33.2 x 52.4 cm, National Gallery of Canada, Ottawa.
Fig 96 (BELOW) William Raphael, *Throwing the Bait, River St. Charles, Quebec*, 1895, oil on canvas, 43.2 x 68.6 cm, private collection.

Significance & Critical Issues

Fig 97 William Raphael, *Portrait of Wolf Rafalsky*, c.1880, oil on canvas, 45.1 x 36.8 cm, collection of Jonathan Wener, Montreal.

William Raphael brought a distinctive vision to his adopted home of Montreal, capturing its people and landscapes with remarkable sensitivity. As the first Jewish artist to build a professional career in Canada, he formed deep connections within his community while also moving through broader cultural circles, including the Freemasons. A key figure in the development of genre painting in Canada, Raphael used everyday scenes to reflect the country's evolving identity. But his prominence as an artist and teacher clashed with shifting aesthetic tastes in Montreal's top art institutions. Coupled with a rising tide of anti-Semitism in the late nineteenth century, these tensions contributed to obscuring Raphael's legacy—despite his pivotal role in shaping Canadian art.

Fig 98 James Duncan, *Jew's Synagogue*, 1839, etching, 17.6 x 10.5 cm, McCord Stewart Museum, Montreal.

Canada's First Jewish Artist

In the first half of the nineteenth century, a population boom in the Prussian Empire led to a vast wave of emigration between 1845 and 1858.[1] William Raphael was one of many Prussians to leave their homeland in search of a better future and fresh opportunities elsewhere. North America was attractive to many Europeans thinking of emigrating. German-language newspapers of the time described the United States and Canada as civilized places with great potential for economic development and a strong emphasis on rights and freedoms.[2] The United States was a popular destination for immigrants, but Raphael was one of the few members of the Prussian community who chose to build a new life in British North America.[3] Arriving in Montreal in 1857, he was the first Jewish artist to immigrate to Canada.[4] His religion marked his career and his work.

Raised in an Orthodox Jewish household in Nakel, Prussia, Raphael produced a number of sketches over the course of his life that reflected his religious upbringing. In October 1856, for example, he drew a figure wearing the tefillin, a small square box containing passages from the Torah.[5] In 1880, years after his arrival in Canada, he painted *Portrait of Wolf Rafalsky*, c.1880 (fig. 97), an image of his father as an austere-looking old man dressed in black, with a beard, curly sideburns, and a yarmulke.

Raphael came of age in an era of greater religious freedom. In fact, at the beginning of the nineteenth century, Prussia passed a number of laws to allow for the emancipation of the Jews and grant them equal rights. When he left Nakel for Berlin at the age of eighteen, Raphael discovered a city marked by these transformations. They carried with them the possibility of a regenerated society and of the potential integration "of the Jewish population with the non-Jewish majority in all domains with the exception of religious life."[6] The mid-nineteenth century was also characterized by a reform movement in Judaism that increasingly guided new generations. Many younger Jews distanced themselves from the age-old traditions that had weighed heavily on the way of life in the past. These cultural changes shaped Raphael's relationship with religion and society throughout his adult life, and in part enabled him to pursue a career as an artist.

In North America, Raphael was part of a new environment, less influenced by religion. Still, his early interactions with Montreal society were initially with his fellow Jewish citizens. On his arrival in the Province of Canada, he joined the city's only synagogue, the Spanish and Portuguese Synagogue, which followed the Orthodox tradition (fig. 98, 100).[7] In 1862, his marriage was celebrated by Rabbi Abraham de Sola,[8] whose portrait Raphael painted on two occasions.[9] In the early years of his career, he also made several portraits for members of his community—notably *Portrait of an Orthodox Jew*, 1861 (fig. 99, 111). Much later, he completed his *Portrait of Aaron Hart David, M.D.*, 1882.[10]

But Raphael did not limit himself to this market alone, nor did he rely solely on the support of his fellow Jews, if only for reasons of economic survival. According to the census, Montreal had a Jewish population of only 181 people in 1851 and 403 in

Fig 99 William Raphael, *Portrait of an Orthodox Jew*, 1861, graphite on paper, 17.8 x 15.2 cm, collection of Jonathan Wener, Montreal.

1861. In the years that followed, this population remained stagnant, with the number barely reaching 409 in 1871.[11] Given this demographic reality, Raphael could not afford to isolate himself, and like his Jewish compatriots, he worked hard to forge links with many people, regardless of their religious affiliation.

By the 1850s and 1860s, he was well integrated into Canadian society. His faith was never mentioned in the newspapers and didn't seem to have the slightest bearing on people's assessment of his skills. He also worked hard to separate his professional life from his religious identity, which he expressed only in private settings.[12] As art historians Loren Lerner and Suzanne Rackover note: "Although active in Montreal's fledgling Jewish community and identified as the first Jewish artist in Canada, Raphael did not produce Jewish-themed art. Rather, he integrated himself into the city's art scene in both subject matter and style."[13]

From the 1880s onwards, however, the artist became more overt about his involvement with the Montreal Jewish community. He also made sure to use his art in activities that supported the Jewish people. For example, in 1882, Raphael donated one of his paintings to a fundraising event dedicated to the construction of the new Temple Emanu-El, which promoted Reform Judaism.[14] In 1892, he also financially supported the Baron de Hirsch Institute (fig. 101), which took in many Jewish migrants, especially Russians and Romanians fleeing persecution in their home countries.[15] Three years later, an article published in the *Gazette* reported on Raphael's life-size portrait of Julius Schermann, which was unveiled during a major ceremony.[16] The work helped to highlight the exceptional efforts of his sitter, who for twelve years served on the board of directors of the Baron de Hirsch Institute and also devoted himself to helping the community's poor as vice-president of the Young Men's Hebrew Benevolent Society.[17]

Despite his increasing public involvement in the Jewish community in the late 1800s, Raphael still did not generally incorporate elements of his religious identity into his works made for the Montreal market, particularly his genre scenes. One notable exception, though, can be found in *With the Current*, 1892 (fig. 94). In that piece, the male figure is dressed in black and wears a yarmulke, leaving no doubt as to his Jewish faith.

Canadian Freemasonry

When William Raphael settled in Montreal in 1857, he integrated into his new environment with the help of his connections in the Jewish community, but he also called on his various other social circles, including the Freemasons. Established in Canada in the eighteenth century, the Masons expanded quickly in the years after the first provincial lodge was set up by the British following the capture of Quebec in 1759.[18] As indicated in the *Freemason's Manual*, written by Thomas Sargant and published in Toronto in 1880, members viewed the fraternal order as "a moral institution, established by virtuous men with the praiseworthy design of recalling to our remembrance the most sublime TRUTHS, in the midst of the most innocent and social pleasures,—founded on LIBERALITY, LOVE and CHARITY."[19]

Fig 100 (ABOVE) Antique wooden ark in the sanctuary at the Spanish and Portuguese Synagogue, Montreal, 2018, photograph by Dave Sidaway / *Montreal Gazette*. **Fig 101** (BELOW) Illustrated postcard of Baron de Hirsch School and Institute, Montreal, c.1903–6, Bibliothèque et Archives nationales du Québec, Montreal. In 1890, the institute was located at 7 rue Sainte-Élizabeth. It moved to a new building on rue de Bleury (pictured above) in 1902.

Fig 102 (LEFT) John Henry Walker, *Thomas Douglas Harington*, 1850–85, ink on paper, relief print, 23.7 x 15.4 cm, McCord Stewart Museum, Montreal. **Fig 103** (RIGHT) William Notman, *W.B. Simpson, Montreal, QC, 1865*, 1865, silver halide on paper mounted on paper, albumen process, 8.5 x 5.6 cm, McCord Stewart Museum, Montreal.

But as the history of Freemasonry shows, not everyone was convinced of these good intentions. Indeed, because of its initiation practices and its secret rituals, as well as the fact that it welcomes members of different faiths, Freemasonry has been condemned in various countries and has especially attracted the wrath of the Catholic Church.[20] As early as 1738, Pope Clement XII, who viewed Masons as heretics and occultists, prohibited Catholics from joining the order.[21] In England and Scotland, on the other hand, Freemasonry was well established and accepted. It experienced an entirely different kind of development in Britain, and eventually in Canada as well. Despite the watchful eye of the Church, new members were recruited year after year and encouraged to take part in the society's meetings.

Raphael was introduced to the Masonic movement by his father-in-law, Hermann Danziger, shortly after his marriage. On March 15, 1864, Danziger nominated his son-in-law for membership, and on April 19, Raphael became a first-degree Freemason.[22] A month later, on May 17, he wrote in his sketchbook that he was "very excited" because he had gone "that evening to the lodge where [he] received [his] second degree as freemason,"[23] thus passing from apprentice to companion and vowing to keep his activities secret. As the society is renowned for its discretion, Raphael left few written clues as to his role within it. But it's worth wondering what he might have gained from such a membership.

Of course, Raphael was not the only Canadian artist to join the order. In Quebec, Freemasonry was sometimes looked upon with suspicion, particularly among Catholics,[24] but nonetheless, some artists—such as François Beaucourt (1740–1794) and Ludger Larose (1868–1915)[25]—were members. Larose was even appointed Master of the only exclusively French-speaking Masonic lodge in Canada, Montreal's Loge des Coeurs-Unis, founded in 1870.

From the outset, the society sought to bring together "educated, active, ambitious men,"[26] holding prestigious positions in civil society and with a taste for the sciences and liberal arts. In Raphael's case, Freemasonry's openness to all religious denominations—including Judaism[27]—allowed him to make contact more easily with many of Montreal's most wealthy and influential figures. In this way, the society offered him an opportunity to penetrate a cultured and stimulating environment and build a network with international scope.

The Masons of Montreal also sponsored a variety of works. For example, Raphael's contemporary, engraver John Henry Walker (1831–1899), was commissioned to make a portrait of Thomas Douglas Harington, the First Grand Principal of the Grand Chapter of Masons of the Royal Arch of Canada (fig. 102). And in 1865, William Notman (1826–1891) photographed Grand Master William B. Simpson wearing the apron of the Brother Masons (fig. 103). That portrait was commissioned by the Grand Lodge of Ancient and Accepted Masons of Canada, and they recorded the expense in their proceedings.[28] Notman and Henry Sandham (1842–1910) also produced a composite image, *Prince Consort and Freemasons Group*, from photographs taken by James Weston (1841–1922) in 1877 (fig. 104). Although he died in 1861, Prince

Fig 104 Notman & Sandham, after James Weston, *Prince Consort and Freemasons Group, 1877*, 1877, silver salts on paper mounted on paper, albumen process, 20.3 x 25.4 cm, McCord Stewart Museum, Montreal.

Fig 105 (LEFT) William Raphael, *Portrait of Jeremiah Wright Wilson*, 1878, oil on canvas, 59 x 48 cm, Galerie de l'Université de Montréal. **Fig 106** (RIGHT) William Raphael, *Portrait of William McGillivray*, 1908, oil on canvas, 77 x 61.3 cm, Château Ramezay, Montreal.

Albert, Queen Victoria's husband, is seated in the front row, at the centre of the composition, in a lodge crowded with brother Masons. The work thus highlights the important networks that connected the secret society and the spheres of power in the nineteenth century.

For Raphael, Masonry afforded the opportunity to develop social networks that undoubtedly played a role in his professional rise and allowed him to win certain artistic commissions. For example, in the 1870s, he offered his services to a prominent member of the brotherhood and created a portrait of Jeremiah Wright Wilson, the Grand Master of Iowa (fig. 105). Wilson is shown with a tie pin decorated with a gold square and compass on a black background, the most recognizable Masonic motif. In 1908, towards the end of his career, Raphael made a copy of a portrait of William McGillivray, the director of the North West Company and a prominent Freemason, at the request of the Numismatic and Antiquarian Society of Montreal (fig. 106).[29] Although it is difficult today to establish the number of pieces made by Raphael for his fellow Freemasons, the fact remains that his membership helped him forge relationships with the intellectual and cultural elites of the time.

A Decline in Status

By the early 1880s, William Raphael was a major figure on the Montreal and Canadian art scene. Appointed one of the first professors of the Art Association of Montreal (AAM), he was also one of the earliest members of the Royal Canadian Academy of Arts (RCA). Some of his works even appeared in prestigious publications, including the book *Picturesque Canada*, published in 1882. This recognition quickly faded, however. In the space of just a few years, Raphael lost his teaching contracts at the AAM (in 1883), failed to obtain financial support from the Royal Canadian Academy despite repeated requests (as early as 1884), and above all, found himself at the centre of a controversy sparked by the Art Association of Montreal (in 1886).

Raphael's decline in status coincided with significant changes in his social circles. Indeed, the painter lost two major supporters in 1882 and 1883. Henry Sandham, a close friend and member of the AAM, left Canada for the United States at the end of 1882,[30] and the Marquess of Lorne, who had bought one of Raphael's works for his personal collection, finished his term as governor general in 1883 and left Canada to take up new duties elsewhere in the British Empire.[31] The departure of these allies happened alongside the rise of a new generation of artists and educators, led by painters Robert Harris (1849–1919) and William Brymner (1855–1925). Because of their recent academic training in Paris, these artists were said to be invigorating Montreal's cultural scene. Though he had worked in Canada for more than twenty years, Raphael was soon seen as part of the old guard, which was slowly being relegated to the background. He often found himself at odds with Harris and Brymner as significant tensions began to form.

In 1883, Robert Harris moved to Montreal and became a professor at the AAM's art school.[32] Raphael, who had been active in art education for many years and had taught the first courses at the AAM, was passed over in favour of him. A rivalry ensued as Raphael began offering courses in his own studio. Newspapers played their part by reporting on the number of students attending each artist's classes and critiquing their works on display. When Harris decided to leave his position at the AAM, he supported the candidacy of his friend William Brymner (fig. 107). Brymner, who took over from Harris in 1885, also had to contend with the success of Raphael's studio, which had moved the previous year to a space just a few steps from the Art Association. From then on, Brymner never hesitated to use his influence with the RCA to block Raphael's requests for financial support.[33]

In this tense climate, the AAM even openly attacked Raphael. In 1886, the *Gazette* reported a discussion about the painter between William Townley Benson, one of Raphael's pupils, and the secretary of the Art Association of Montreal, a Mr. English. The conversation went like this:

> "Raphael, being a teacher, cannot be expected to paint, besides he never had any education except what he got in Notman's studio, painting photographs. All the pictures which he has sent to the gallery for the last few years have been failures." When pressed as to whether Raphael ever studied in Europe, he [Mr. English] replied, "Oh yes, I believe he did, for a few months in Düsseldorf, the worst school, the worst school in Europe."
>
> I [Benson] said Raphael studied in Berlin, at the Academy. "Berlin was it?" said he, "well, it is six of one and half a dozen of the other." Much more was said in the same strain, but the foregoing is sufficient for the purpose.[34]

Apart from the mockery, the secretary of the AAM had shamefully belittled Raphael's training, as well as his work. Efforts to discredit Raphael were persistent and long-lasting. At the beginning of the following century, in 1904, the *Daily Witness* devoted a long article to the history of the AAM school in which Raphael was only briefly mentioned. The text states that in 1881, "an experimental series of advanced art classes was established under the supervision of a committee, taught by Mr. Raphael, Mr. Edson, Mr. Van Luppen."[35] In other words, in the official narrative of this aspect of art history, Raphael (fig. 108) is barely named and his pioneering work as a teacher is framed as an experiment under the supervision of a committee. The journalist never explains why these three men were not asked back to teach at the institution. Instead, he gives all the credit for setting up the school to Robert Harris and, above all, William Brymner.

Facing the Rise of Anti-Semitism

William Raphael's loss of influence in the early 1880s may not have been entirely due to artistic issues and struggles for prestige among various players. Prejudice may also have played a role in sidelining the artist.[36] The climate in Canada was coloured by world events. In Russia, the assassination of Tsar Alexander II in 1881 by a revolutionary group called the Will of the People ushered in a new period of anti-Jewish

Fig 107 (ABOVE) William Brymner with his students at the Art Association of Montreal, 1902, photographer unknown. **Fig 108** (BELOW) William Raphael, painter, c.1890, photographer unknown, McCord Stewart Museum, Montreal.

Fig 109 (LEFT) Rogers Arnott & Sauer, *Interior of English, German, and Polish Synagogue on McGill College Avenue*, 1890, composite photograph, 24.6 x 18.7 cm, Congregation Shaar Hashomayim Museum and Archives, Montreal. **Fig 110** (RIGHT) Wm. Notman & Son, *Shaar Hashomayim Synagogue, 59 McGill College Avenue, Montreal, QC, about 1910–11*, c.1910–11, silver salts on glass, gelatin dry plate process, 25.4 x 20.3 cm, McCord Stewart Museum, Montreal.

sentiment.[37] The murder, falsely attributed to Jewish terrorists, led to waves of violence (pogroms) and the introduction of discriminatory laws.[38] The Jews of the Russian Empire fled in droves—more than two million of them were forced into exile.[39]

Canada welcomed such a large number of refugees that its Jewish population jumped from 2,443 in 1881 to 6,501 in 1891.[40] In Montreal, the increase was particularly noticeable, with the population of Jewish people rising from 814 to 2,473 over the same ten-year period.[41] And the numbers continued to grow. In the Canadian census of 1901, 16,401 Jewish people lived in Canada, nearly 40 percent of them in Montreal.[42] The massive influx of Jews from Europe in the last twenty years of the nineteenth century changed the spiritual landscape of the city. Until the end of the nineteenth century, Montreal had been home to a small Jewish community adapted to the British colonial way of life. The community is reflected in a composite photograph showing worshippers at the English, German, and Polish synagogue on McGill College Avenue, a temple belonging to one of Canada's oldest Jewish congregations (the Shaar Hashomayim congregation, founded in Montreal in 1846) (fig. 109–110). In this bright and airy space, the male members wear top hats and sport moustaches and beards in the style of the time.

The massive migration of Jewish people in the 1880s also corresponded to the resurgence of prejudices on an international scale, which in turn undermined their integration into Canada. This situation was exploited by people like the British Canadian historian and journalist Goldwin Smith (1823–1910), who had been a professor at Oxford and Cornell University before he settled in Toronto in 1871, and thus enjoyed a high status in intellectual circles. Smith disparaged Jews as an unpatriotic, inward-looking people who were corrupting the greatness of a country that should, first and foremost, embody Anglo-Saxon values.[43] He constantly advanced the view that the growing numbers of Jews in North America threatened the Anglo-Saxon way of life and Canada's religious equilibrium.

As early as 1878, Smith was publishing anti-Semitic articles and giving speeches in both Canada and the United States in support of his point of view.[44] By 1891, he was describing the Jewish people as a parasitic race.[45] According to Smith, who cloaked his bigotry in academic language, all Jews, no matter where they were born—Russia, England, or the United States—possessed the same so-called racial characteristics, regardless of their social or intellectual abilities.[46] Although his ideas were criticized by some, they nonetheless found an audience in Canada during this time of increasing prejudice and discrimination.[47]

This rhetoric undoubtedly affected William Raphael. He saw the religious and racial tolerance that had allowed him to lead a fairly serene life in Canada collapsing before his eyes. Seemingly overnight, he could no longer count on the same benevolent support from the Canadian cultural community. Smith's screeds about the threats to Anglo-Saxon superiority were reflected in Raphael's loss of his teaching position at the Art Association of Montreal (AAM). Indeed, in 1882, the institution decided that its courses would be organized in accordance with the British model, which the

Fig 111 William Raphael, *Portrait of an Orthodox Jew Smoking*, 1861, oil on canvas, 31.1 x 26 cm, collection of Jonathan Wener, Montreal.

Fig 112 William Raphael, *Portrait of Mrs. William Raphael, born Ernestina Danziger*, December 9, 1891, oil on canvas, 63.5 x 50.2 cm, collection of Jonathan Wener, Montreal.

Fig 113 William Raphael, *Self-Portrait of the Artist*, c.1885, oil on canvas, 61 x 50.8 cm, collection of Jonathan Wener, Montreal.

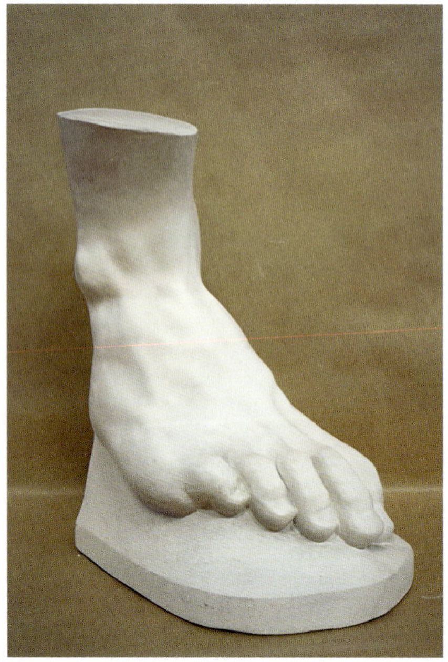

Fig 114 (LEFT) Artist unknown, after Leochares, *Apollo Belvedere, Drawing Model*, second half of the nineteenth century, plaster and paint, unknown dimensions, unknown location. **Fig 115** (RIGHT) Artist unknown, *Right Foot, Drawing Model*, second half of the nineteenth century, plaster, unknown dimensions, unknown location.

AAM's board of directors considered to be the best in the world. Attempts were even made to recruit a London-based teacher, without success.[48] In the end, the institution came to favour English-speaking painters with undeniable British roots.

Against this backdrop arose a "genteel" anti-Semitism, to use the term proposed by historian Alan Mendelson.[49] As he demonstrates in his book *Exiles from Nowhere*, this form of anti-Semitism was adopted by some members of Canada's English-speaking elite, whose notions of decorum and "gentlemanliness" encouraged a subtle racism over more brutal gestures.[50] This led many Jews to quietly withdraw from their wider social and cultural circles. In the last quarter of the nineteenth century, imperialist thinking, racial animus, and anti-Semitism found a place in Victorian society.

The words and actions of people like Goldwin Smith meant that a Jewish painter like Raphael was not as welcome as before (fig. 112–113).[51] His religious identity overshadowed his artistic abilities, which no longer seemed to be considered objectively. He was forced to give up the fight for public recognition. During the last three decades of his life, the climate was simply not favourable.

A Teacher of Art

Raphael's significant contributions to the history of art in Canada are especially reflected in his involvement in art education. In the 1860s, he taught classes in his own studio, at a time when Montreal had no art schools. He also started teaching art to the Sisters of Sainte-Anne in 1879, and to the nuns of the Congrégation de Notre-Dame around 1883.[52] He was further instrumental in establishing the drawing and painting curriculum at the Art Association of Montreal's art school, and he held positions at the Montreal Society of Decorative Art (in 1881 and between 1883 and 1884), Mrs. Lovell's Educational Institute (in 1884), and the Eliock School (in 1893).[53] In 1896, he also began offering classes at the Art Building in Sherbrooke.[54]

Through these avenues, Raphael reached an incalculable number of students over the course of four decades, contributing as much to cultivating a taste for the arts in society as to the training of future artists. This considerable contribution helped to increase the number of art lovers, collectors, and supporters of artistic production in Montreal. Raphael's efforts also nourished the city's cultural life and fostered a better understanding of art among those who lived there.

Raphael favoured a teaching method that largely duplicated the academic model he'd learned from during his training in Berlin. In 1887, the *Montreal Herald and Daily Commercial Gazette*, in a report on an exhibition of work by his pupils, described the exhibition room,[55] giving some insight into his approach:

> [T]he walls are covered with drawings in crayon and charcoal, works by the pupils, consisting of studies from living models, statuary, busts and masks. Particularly fine are the charcoal sketches from life. The various phases of art are here exhibited from the sketches of hands, feet, eyes, etc.[56]

Fig 116 William Raphael, *Hand on Guitar*, January 31, 1854, canvas mounted on cardboard, 24 x 29.5 cm, Musée de Lachine, Montreal.

Fig 117 William Raphael, *Good News*, 1875, oil on canvas laid down on board, 35.6 x 21 cm, collection of Jonathan Wener, Montreal.

Fig 118 William Raphael, *Portrait of a Habitant in Red Tuque*, 1906, oil on canvas, 30.5 x 22.9 cm, collection of Jonathan Wener, Montreal.

Fig 119 William Raphael's painting palette, c.1879–1914, Musée de Lachine, Montreal.

Fig 120 William Raphael, *Moonlight*, 1898, unknown location.

The description illustrates that drawing was the preferred method of artistic instruction, as was the case in the academic system. Pupils began by copying two-dimensional works (engravings, drawings, and paintings by the masters) and then progressed to observing static three-dimensional objects (statues, bas-reliefs), and ultimately moved to drawing from a live model. Each stage allowed for the development of the artist's skill and emphasized composition and tonal variation.

For the first stage, copying two-dimensional models, the teacher would show his pupils various examples, including his own work. In fact, some of Raphael's pieces, such as a painting of a hand dated January 31, 1854 (fig. 116), show small holes in the corners—a sign that they had been pinned up several times to be used as studies. Raphael also instructed his pupils to draw plaster models from his own collection. Many of these objects were preserved when they were sold in 1910 to the Sisters of Sainte-Anne.[57] Some correspond to ancient figures, such as the bust of the *Apollo Belvedere* (fig. 114). Others show only a fragment of the body, to allow students to practise detail work (fig. 115).

Once his pupils had developed basic skills, Raphael had them do exercises with live models. As he explained to the *Herald* reporter, these sessions were long, since "for the completed picture the models generally have to give four sittings of three hours each"[58] It's not clear whether models posed nude, as was the custom in the academic system. Given the strong influence of religion in Quebec at the time, it is more likely that they were clothed.

Most of the sitters brought into Raphael's studio were male, and although we don't know their names, some appear across the painter's body of work. Sometime in the mid-1870s, for example, Raphael created a bust-length portrait of a warmly dressed man posed in front of an interior background.[59] The same man appears in *Good News*, a later composition from 1875 (fig. 117). In this work, the man stands near a street lamp holding the latest editions of the *Daily Witness* and the *Evening Star*. Several years later, the model posed again, for a work in which he's shown with aged features, wearing a red tuque and smoking a pipe (fig. 118).

Raphael also taught painting classes, but it's evident from the 1887 *Herald* article that these lessons were designed for his more advanced students.[60] The two main genres of these classes were landscape and still life. Many of Raphael's pupils created copies of his own compositions in both—one notable example is a landscape painting copied by Sister Marie-Hélène-de-la-Croix (née Élisabeth Martin, 1861–1956) of the Sisters of Sainte-Anne.[61] A fundamental exercise in the academic system, copying allowed for deeper understanding of technique. This pedagogical approach helped Raphael's students better recognize subtleties in colour harmonies. In his teaching, he used colour palettes as references, and one of these palettes, which bears the words "night" and "moon," corresponds to the range of hues used in his landscapes, including *Moonlight*, 1898 (fig. 119–120).

Raphael was one of the first teachers in Canada to give outdoor painting classes. He encouraged the direct contemplation of nature and the desire to capture its fleeting effects, and he told his students to "[o]bserve nature carefully, especially the delicate cloud formations and aerial perspectives."[62] In this way, he reminded them to pay attention to the landscape through their encounter with it. The *Herald* article notes that the landscapes on display in the exhibition of his pupils' work were made "from nature"—perhaps a reference to *plein air* painting. This method does appear to have been a component of Raphael's teaching, as evidenced by *A Sketch from Nature* (fig. 50), a scene in which he depicts one of his students during an outdoor painting session at the Black River in 1882.[63] Ten years later, his pupils at the Sisters of Sainte-Anne noted that they had practised *plein air* painting under Raphael's instruction.[64]

The *Montreal Herald and Daily Commercial Gazette* article also emphasizes Raphael's use of the still life as a teaching tool. He undoubtedly had plaster reproductions of various foods and flowers, as a way of ensuring that these items didn't perish between sessions. Although Raphael didn't produce many still-life compositions in his own practice, some of his depictions of flowers show a familiarity with plaster models (fig. 121). In 1880, the *Gazette* reported that he had just finished several paintings of fish and birds.[65] *Still Life (Northern Flickers)*, 1885, offers a glimpse into Raphael's skill with the genre: it is a *trompe l'oeil* showing two dead birds suspended by their legs in front of a wooden surface (fig. 122). A composition depicting fish, signed by Sister Marie-Hélène-de-la-Croix, demonstrates how Raphael's still-life paintings could serve as models for his students (fig. 123).

While based on the academic model and its system of progressive learning, Raphael's educational program was rich and varied, incorporating practices inside and outside of the classroom to give pupils direct access to some of the most important methods for studying and creating art during the nineteenth century.

Fig 121 William Raphael, *Still Life with Blossoms*, May 24, 1886, oil on board, 24.8 x 20.3 cm, collection of Jonathan Wener, Montreal.

Legacy

Apart from six references in the second edition of art historian Dennis Reid's *A Concise History of Canadian Painting* (1988), William Raphael is scarcely mentioned in most overviews of Canadian art history. But he played a key role in the country's cultural life that went well beyond producing his major work, *Behind Bonsecours Market, Montreal*, 1866 (fig. 63). He also opened up creative avenues that supported the artists who followed him.

Raphael played a dynamic role in the artistic community of his time. He was one of the few people in Montreal who saw the value in organizations capable of professionalizing the visual arts, exhibiting works, and training the next generations of artists, and he was a key figure in the founding of both the Art Association of Montreal and the Canadian Academy of Art (later the Royal Canadian Academy of Arts). He contributed to these organizations in palpable ways by exhibiting his work, teaching their courses, and sitting on their committees. In this way, he bolstered these essential institutions and all they represented for many years.

Perhaps most importantly, Raphael established an artistic practice that had a major impact on the history of Canadian art. Along with his contemporaries Cornelius Krieghoff (1815–1872) and James Duncan (1806–1881), he was one of the first Canadian

Fig 122 William Raphael, *Still Life (Northern Flickers)*, 1885, oil on paper, mounted on pressed paper fibreboard, 46.5 x 31.5 cm, National Gallery of Canada, Ottawa.

Fig 123 Sister Marie-Hélène-de-la-Croix, *Sea Trout* (*Truites saumonées*), 1893, oil on canvas, 68.7 x 46 cm, Musée de Lachine, Montreal.

Fig 124 William Raphael, *Gathering Wood in Winter*, c.1880–1914, oil on canvas, 43.2 x 33.1 cm, collection of Jonathan Wener, Montreal.

Fig 125 William Raphael, *Royal Mail, New Brunswick*, 1861, oil on canvas, 30.5 x 35.6 cm, Beaverbrook Art Gallery, Fredericton.

Fig 126 William Raphael, *Habitant*, c.1872–1910, oil on canvas, 35.9 x 28.3 cm, collection of Jonathan Wener, Montreal.

Fig 127 Alfred Laliberté, *The Cedar Match*, from the Trades, Customs and Legends of Yesteryear series, 1927–31, bronze, 36.7 x 49.6 x 24.3 cm, Musée national des beaux-arts du Québec, Quebec City.

artists to explore the theme of nordicity, or northernness (fig. 124). Blizzards, hoods, and tuques were part of his repertoire from his very first years in Canada. A case in point is *Royal Mail, New Brunswick*, 1861 (fig. 125), which depicts a warmly dressed coachman at the head of a sleigh drawn by four horses on a snowy road. Long before painters like Maurice Cullen (1866–1934) and A.Y. Jackson (1882–1974), he recognized the strong role Canada's northern landscape played in defining the country.

Raphael also showed a great interest in depicting traditional Canadian figures. But unlike Krieghoff, who sometimes turned his subjects into caricatures, Raphael opted for a more realistic representation. As early as the 1870s, he had established an image of the French Canadian habitant: a man wearing a tuque and a woven sash, shown in a modest domestic interior furnished with a hooked rug and a stove (fig. 126). In this moment captured in time, Raphael emphasizes local details and creates a compositional formula that, many years later, would be echoed in the works of Marc-Aurèle de Foy Suzor-Coté (1869–1937) and Alfred Laliberté (1877–1953) (fig. 127).

Finally, much of the credit for promoting the artistic potential of the Charlevoix region belongs to William Raphael, who painted the area more than thirty years before Clarence Gagnon (1881–1942) popularized it. Since the end of the eighteenth century, the Charlevoix had been captured by the pens and paintbrushes of British military watercolourists such as James Peachey (d.1797) and George Bulteel Fisher (1764–1837), but it was still rarely visited by other artists.[66] In fact, it wasn't until the middle of the nineteenth century that the region began to attract more painters, including Raphael (fig. 128). In 1869, when the *Quebec Daily Mercury* newspaper interviewed him on his return from a summer trip, he praised the Charlevoix in glowing terms, referring to it as the "Switzerland of Canada."[67]

Following this trip, he completed a painting entitled *Falls of le Trou*, which he exhibited at the second Society of Canadian Artists exhibition, held in early 1870.[68] He then made further trips to Murray Bay (La Malbaie), notably in 1878 and 1887.[69] Unlike many Canadian artists of the 1880s, who favoured the landscapes of Western Canada and the Rocky Mountains, Raphael instead discovered an inspiring place, worthy of his greatest creations, in Quebec. The Charlevoix region was so important to him that when he was seeking membership in the newly founded Canadian Academy of Arts in 1880, he chose as his reception piece *Indian Encampment on the Lower St. Lawrence Estuary*, 1879 (fig. 84), a majestic landscape depicting Murray Bay. In 1881, he chose another landscape from this same location, *Scene at Murray Bay*, to be reproduced and included in a portfolio compiled by the Art Association of Montreal and distributed to all its members.[70] In his own way, he helped people see the intrinsic beauty of these sites through an artistic eye.

Fig 128 William Raphael, *Murray Bay Rock in Greenery*, 1878, 43 x 30 cm, oil on cardboard, Musée de Lachine, Montreal.

Style & Technique

MONTREAL
W. RAPHAEL

William Raphael was a pioneer in bringing a refined realism to Canadian art, shaped by the Biedermeier tradition he absorbed during his formative years in Berlin. His meticulous attention to detail and commitment to capturing life as it appeared placed him at the forefront of a shift in artistic practice. This emphasis on observational precision dovetailed with the emergence of photography, a medium that was transforming how people perceived and represented the world. Raphael also embraced plein air *painting, working directly in nature to bring a sense of immediacy and vitality to his landscapes. His compositions often include touches of wit, revealing a personal warmth and underscoring the depth and diversity of his artistic voice.*

Fig 129 (OPPOSITE PAGE) William Raphael, *Going to Town*, 1862, oil on canvas, 30.5 x 35.2 cm, RiverBrink Art Museum, Niagara-on-the-Lake, Ontario. **Fig 130** (ABOVE) Unknown artist, after William Raphael, *St. Jean-Baptiste Parade Outside the Montreal Bank, 1872*, 1932, silver salts on paper, gelatin silver process, 19 x 24 cm, McCord Stewart Museum, Montreal. **Fig 131** (BELOW) Franz Krüger, *Parade on the Opernplatz, Berlin, 1822*, 1829, oil on canvas, 249 x 374 cm, Alte Nationalgalerie, Berlin.

Bringing Biedermeier to Canada

William Raphael's student years in Berlin were marked by one of the most important artistic currents in the Prussian Empire, the Biedermeier movement,[1] which influenced the visual arts, design, and music. Generally spanning the years between 1815 (the Congress of Vienna) and 1848 (the Springtime of Nations), the Biedermeier period originated in the German-speaking cities of Berlin, Munich, and Vienna, before spreading to Scandinavia and the Russian Empire (notably Copenhagen and St. Petersburg).[2] During the first half of the nineteenth century, artists of this movement looked beyond traditional academic teaching. Instead of focusing on historical subjects (ancient, mythological, religious) and models derived from Greco-Roman statuary, they wanted to address the realities of their environment and engage their art in a relationship with everyday life.[3] In the words of art historian Geraldine Norman, "[R]ealism, the faithful and objective rendering of nature, is the essence of Biedermeier painting."[4] The result is an approach tinged with reality and a preference for genre scenes, portraits, and landscapes. Several of Raphael's works—such as *The Old Pedlar*, 1859 (fig. 18); *Haymarket Square / Victoria Square*, 1861 (fig. 60); *Going to Town*, 1862 (fig. 129); *Bonsecours Market*, 1864 (fig. 24); and *Behind Bonsecours Market, Montreal*, 1866 (fig. 63)—illustrate this approach. In these paintings, he takes care to capture the scenes in minute detail.

Raphael's *St. Jean-Baptiste Parade Outside the Montreal Bank*, 1872 (fig. 130), is reminiscent of *Parade on the Opernplatz, Berlin, 1822*, 1829 (fig. 131), by German Biedermeier

Fig 132 (ABOVE) Otto Reinhold Jacobi, *The Rapids, Montmorency River* (*Les Rapides, rivière Montmorency*), 1860, oil on canvas, 41 x 48.8 cm, Musée national des beaux-arts du Québec, Quebec City. **Fig 133** (BELOW) Adolphe Vogt, *Niagara Falls*, 1869, oil on canvas, 51 x 99.2 cm, National Gallery of Canada, Ottawa.

Fig 134 (LEFT) Jules-Ernest Livernois, *Honoré Mercier*, c.1880, acetate negative, 25 x 20 cm, Bibliothèque et Archives nationales du Québec, Montreal. **Fig 135** (RIGHT) William Raphael, *Portrait of Louis-Édouard Desjardins*, 1877, oil on canvas, 67 x 53.5 cm, Pointe-à-Callière, Montreal Archaeology and History Complex.

painter Franz Krüger (1797–1857).[5] Both paintings demonstrate a desire to capture a severe architectural setting where light abounds. The urban landscapes where the action unfolds are vividly depicted, and in both works, the characters' clothes and activities are carefully rendered to preserve a sense of realism.

In many respects, Raphael's Biedermeier roots and German training resulted in an approach reminiscent of the work of compatriots who settled in Canada after him. The spirit of the Biedermeier movement can especially be seen in pieces by Otto Reinhold Jacobi (1812–1901) and Adolphe Vogt (1842–1871). Before arriving in Canada, Jacobi studied at the Royal Academy of Arts in Berlin and then at the Düsseldorf Academy, where he developed his technique under the guidance of landscape painter Johann Wilhelm Schirmer (1807–1863), who was closely associated with the Biedermeier movement.[6] Vogt was trained at the Munich Academy by animal painter Rudolf Koller (1828–1905).

When Jacobi settled in Montreal in 1860, he immediately befriended Raphael. His landscapes, such as *The Rapids, Montmorency River*, 1860 (fig. 132), sought to capture reality by meticulously depicting details like the rock strata of this natural setting. Vogt, who joined his family in Montreal in 1865, also demonstrated an adherence to Biedermeier principles in his work.[7] His paintings from the 1860s, such as *Niagara Falls*, 1869 (fig. 133), express a vision primarily rooted in realism, the pursuit of natural effects, and an interest in creating minor genres. Through art linked to the aesthetics then in vogue in the Prussian Empire, Raphael, Jacobi, and Vogt brought a distinct approach to Canadian painting and helped to revitalize the cultural environment in the years leading up to Confederation.[8]

Photography for Pictorial Purposes

Raphael was still a boy when the first photographic process, the daguerreotype, was introduced in 1839. The invention made it technically possible to capture reality as it unfolds before the camera lens. By the time Raphael had completed his training in Berlin and settled in Montreal in 1857, photography had become an increasingly popular means of expression. The connections between painting and photography were obvious: many photographers first trained as painters, and many painters worked for professional photographers in their studios, creating backgrounds and so on.

By 1859, Raphael had already started to work with William Notman (1826–1891), and he later worked with Abner Bedee Taber (1832–1866) and James Inglis (1835–1904) as well. Raphael may have even collaborated with Quebec City photographer Jules-Ernest Livernois (1851–1933) on a portrait of politician Honoré Mercier produced around 1890 (fig. 134).[9]

As part of his work in the Notman studio, Raphael created a number of portraits from black-and-white photographic enlargements. In this process, the photograph becomes the equivalent of a preparatory drawing that an artist traces on his canvas before applying colour. Working from the enlarged photograph, the painter colours the surface, taking care to preserve the details of the original piece. Photography

Fig 136 William Notman Studio, *Sir Robert Abercromby and W. Dudgeon, Montreal, QC, 1876*, 1876, silver salts on paper mounted on paper, 12.7 x 17.8 cm, McCord Stewart Museum, Montreal.

Fig 137 William Raphael, *Sledding, Fletcher's Field, Montreal*, 1875–78, graphite on wove paper, 9.4 x 14.6 cm, National Gallery of Canada, Ottawa.

transformed the hours a sitter might once have spent immobilized in the painter's studio into a few minutes in front of the camera lens. The painter could then copy the photographic portrait onto canvas at leisure, without worrying that the subject would change his or her pose. This approach resulted in meticulously rendered pictorial works like *The McFarlane Children*, 1871 (fig. 74), and *Portrait of Louis-Édouard Desjardins*, 1877 (fig. 135).

For Raphael, photography was not just a tool that facilitated his work as a portraitist but also a medium that perfectly aligned with his Biedermeier principles.[10] The image captured by the lens reflected a reality that was a foundation of his artistic approach. What's more, the collaborative work of painters and photographers facilitated the development of subjects and techniques that had not yet been widely explored in art.

In the 1870s, for example, Notman developed composite photography, a multi-stage process for assembling many photographs on a single surface. The method allowed him to produce images that bypassed the technical limitations of the camera—in particular, slow shutter speeds that made it impossible to catch subjects in motion. At a time when the technology to capture and stop action instantaneously did not exist, Notman devised a solution by taking shots in the studio and then having his art department cut and paste them onto a background. The portrait of Sir Robert Abercromby and W. Dudgeon, for example, was the result of a collaborative effort between Notman and the members of his art department, including painter Henry Sandham (1842–1910) (fig. 136).

This intersection of disciplines led to the development of iconographies that were still relatively uncommon in the visual arts, such as scenes of people tobogganing or bobsledding. Influenced by the work of Notman and his studio, Raphael made a sketch of Fletcher's Field, around 1878, showing many people embracing this winter pastime (fig. 137). We can imagine him observing the scene in the large Montreal park and quickly capturing it in graphite—an approach well suited to expressing the sense of movement implied by such a subject. Two years later, he produced the painting *Bobsledding, Fletcher's Field, Montreal* (fig. 138), and in 1885, a reproduction of his piece *Rural Bliss* appeared in the *Daily Witness*.[11] These two works, showing young people tobogganing in closer detail, are reminiscent of the composite images created by Notman and also reproduced by Sandham in *Tobogganing, Winter Scene in Montreal*, 1885, and Alfred Boisseau (1823–1901) in *La Descente en toboggan*, 1881.[12] By combining

Fig 138 William Raphael, *Bobsledding, Fletcher's Field, Montreal*, 1880, oil on canvas, 45 x 27 cm, collection of Jonathan Wener, Montreal.

Fig 139 William Hogarth, *John Wilkes Esq.*, 1763, etching and engraving; first state of two, 36.4 x 23.4 cm, Metropolitan Museum of Art, New York.

the possibilities offered by photography with his painterly sensibility, Raphael epitomized this hybrid artistic practice, where collaboration between painters and photographers allowed for new subjects and a new way of seeing the world.

A Little Bit of Humour

Raphael was not a caricaturist and his art was not essentially humorous, but he occasionally liked to incorporate light-hearted elements into his work, and these sometimes revealed aspects of his temperament. In fact, many of Raphael's paintings feature smiling characters and scenes of mockery, leading some contemporaries to compare his art to that of William Hogarth (1697–1764) (fig. 139) or Adolf Schrödter (or Schroedter, 1805–1875).

The first clear expression of Raphael's sense of humour came in his early sketchbook (fig. 140–141), and also in the mid-1860s, when he responded to a critical review of his painting *Behind Bonsecours Market, Montreal* by creating a new version that featured, as the *Art Journal of London* put it, "a graphic full-length caricature of a noted *blind Art-critic*, who is a stumbling-block in the way of every artist visiting Montreal."[13] Raphael deliberately used caricature to hit back at his detractors, and seemingly to great success. The critic for the *Art Journal* went on to compare him to "the immortal Hogarth"— high praise indeed, given the popularity of Hogarth's satirical works.[14] But it never became Raphael's habit to use caricature to score points.

Some of his pieces occasionally include humorous touches that call to mind the work of Cornelius Krieghoff (1815–1872). The two artists shared many similarities, particularly in their depictions of Canada and everyday life, and in their appreciation of local culture. Raphael may have been influenced by Krieghoff's work when he produced pieces marked by a similar light-heartedness. At times, he almost seems to be following in the older man's footsteps—his paintings *Tandem*, 1869 and 1878 (fig. 69, 142), for example, seem to evoke Krieghoff's *Sled Race across the Ice*, 1861 (fig. 143). Both works exude the same sense of pleasure in winter activities and are tinged with a childlike, joyful quality.

Parallels with Krieghoff are also evident in *The Early Bird Picks Up the Worm*, 1869 (fig. 67). This piece, which shows two dishevelled men going from door to door in search of food, is notably reminiscent of two 1858 works by Krieghoff: *Pour l'amour du bon dieu?* and *Va au diable!*. These paintings, like Raphael's, were made available on a larger scale through chromolithographic reproduction.[15] The works display similarities in their subjects' facial expressions, the multiple layers of patched clothing, and the titles chosen to enhance the humorous effect.

The lightness of Raphael's work, while more evident in some pieces from the 1860s, didn't vanish into thin air in the challenging decades that followed. In 1886, for example, he exhibited the painting *Never Too Late to Mend*, which, according to a *Montreal Star* journalist, was a good example of his humour.[16]

The titles of two paintings exhibited eleven years apart—*A Bad Case* and *A Difficult Problem*—suggest that Raphael maintained his sense of humour even as his career prospects deteriorated. The first of these, *A Bad Case*, was exhibited at the Art

Fig 140 William Raphael, *Man and Two Women*, August 25, 1851, graphite on wove paper, 15.8 x 10 cm, National Gallery of Canada, Ottawa.

Fig 141 William Raphael, *Head and Figure Studies*, 1850–59, graphite on wove paper, 15.8 x 10 cm, National Gallery of Canada, Ottawa.

Fig 142 William Raphael, *Tandem*, 1878, oil on canvas, 53.3 x 87.6 cm, collection of Jonathan Wener, Montreal.

Fig 143 Cornelius Krieghoff, *Sled Race across the Ice*, 1861, oil on canvas, 36.2 x 53.6 cm, Montreal Museum of Fine Arts.

Fig 144 William Raphael, *Portrait of a Lady*, 1884, oil on millboard, 28 x 22.8 cm, Winnipeg Art Gallery—Qaumajuq.

Fig 145 William Raphael, *Portrait of a Man*, 1874, oil on canvas, 68.6 x 55.9 cm, collection of Jonathan Wener, Montreal.

Association of Montreal in 1887, after he'd been mocked publicly by the secretary of the organization. The painting depicts a tinsmith who refuses to give up his work, even though everything seems hopeless.[17] In 1898, following his resignation from the Royal Canadian Academy of Arts in 1896 after years of failing to obtain financial support, he presented A *Difficult Problem* at its annual exhibition.[18] Even though the title is cloaked in humour, it's difficult not to read it as Raphael's final criticism of this institution.

The Measured Shifts of the Pictorial Language

William Raphael produced a body of work that, taken as a whole, displays a great deal of cohesion in terms of subject matter and pictorial treatment. His portraits, for example, are similar in style at both the beginning and the end of his career. In this respect, he didn't deviate greatly from his training in Berlin. In each portrait he made, he meticulously captured the features of the subject's face, applied a sense of suppleness to the modelling, and chose a colour palette consisting largely of earth tones (fig. 144–145). His backgrounds, in contrast, were often rendered with looser brushwork. This practice didn't change much over the years.

In Raphael's genre scenes and landscapes, the pictorial treatment was different. The figures are not depicted as carefully as they are in his portraits (fig. 146). Instead, the modelling is often simplified and the details executed more hastily. Throughout the 1860s and 1870s, in paintings such as *Haymarket Square / Victoria Square*, 1861 (fig. 60), and *Royal Mail, New Brunswick*, 1861 (fig. 125), Raphael would use a tone-on-tone treatment to render his subjects' clothes, layering a lighter topcoat over a darker base. But he always left room for the imprint of his brush and the texture of the canvas.

In his early landscapes, Raphael often depicted natural elements such as branches, grasses, and water with thinly applied paint—see, for instance, the tree in the composition *Boy and a Cart*, 1860 (fig. 19). In this work, Raphael afforded his brush little freedom to capture the texture of the foliage (fig. 147). A few years later, however, he began to slightly alter his approach. In the painting *Double Barn Building Reflecting in Water*, 1874 (fig. 148), the shrubs along the shoreline reveal multiple brushstrokes—sometimes round, sometimes elongated—left on the surface of the canvas.

By the end of the 1870s, Raphael's pictorial style became lighter. Perhaps influenced by friends who had returned from studying in France and by the new Impressionist movement, he gradually abandoned his earthy palette. Though not a strict follower of Impressionism, he nonetheless began to opt for lighter colours and more visible brushstrokes. In the 1880s, Raphael tried to reflect the luminous atmospheres he encountered on his excursions. The painting *Landscape with Pond and Pink Bushes*, 1885 (fig. 149), captures a cloudy summer scene with much less grey and brown than is found in his works of the preceding decades. The grasses and foliage and the swirls of water show a diversity of colours: greens, oranges, reds, and so on. The clouds in the sky appear to have been rendered with a palette knife, as the paint has been gently crushed and swept over the canvas.

The same type of brushwork, with its many strokes and less precision, can be

Fig 146 William Raphael, *Two Indian Women*, 1873, oil on paper mounted on cardboard, 25 x 18.1 cm, Montreal Museum of Fine Arts.

Fig 147 William Raphael, *Boy and a Cart* (detail), 1860, oil on canvas, 58.4 x 47 cm, collection of Jonathan Wener, Montreal.

Fig 148 William Raphael, *Double Barn Building Reflecting in Water*, 1874, oil on panel, 33 x 48.3 cm, collection of Jonathan Wener, Montreal.

Fig 149 William Raphael, *Landscape with Pond and Pink Bushes*, August 25, 1885, oil on panel, 40.6 x 30.5 cm, collection of Jonathan Wener, Montreal.

Fig 150 William Raphael, *Cowansville*, July 16, 1885, graphite on paper, 12.2 x 16.7 cm, McCord Stewart Museum, Montreal.

seen in other works over the years, both *plein air* pochades (quick sketches) and paintings finished in the studio, such as *An Amateur*, 1886 (fig. 153), and *With the Current*, 1892. Although Raphael didn't fully embrace the emerging Impressionist movement in Canada, he was able to incorporate elements of its style in his work, revealing an ongoing curiosity about exploring different techniques.

From *Plein Air* to the Studio

William Raphael notably kept detailed notebooks throughout his career. These books, filled continually over the years, provide important evidence of his artistic practice. From an early age, he developed a habit of putting his observations down on paper, a practice that became integral as he evolved his artistic approach to encountering nature in his work. The many visual notes he made during trips to Germany and Scotland, as well as to Louiseville, Cowansville (fig. 150), and Montebello in Quebec, reveal his preference for working *en plein air*. Raphael also took advantage of the developing railway infrastructure to get around Quebec, as evidenced by *Waiting for the Train, Dunn Station, Lachine*, 1883 (fig. 151).

In some of his sketches, he wrote notes about the colours he'd observed. He also produced quick paintings in situ, using a small piece of cardboard or a wooden panel as a support. One of the earliest examples of this practice is a landscape of Lake Memphremagog painted in 1869 (fig. 152). In his quest to capture the scene's atmosphere and light effects as quickly as possible, Raphael painted with visible brushstrokes, without attempting to fill the entire surface perfectly. This spontaneous treatment allowed him to catch the fleeting moment of the cloudy scene unfolding before his eyes.

For Raphael, this approach was in keeping with the practice favoured by Biedermeier artists. Johann Wilhelm Schirmer, for example, was famous for spending time

Fig 151 William Raphael, *Waiting for the Train, Dunn Station, Lachine*, June 25, 1883, graphite on paper, 16.6 x 12.2 cm, McCord Stewart Museum, Montreal.

Fig 152 William Raphael, *Untitled (Lake Memphremagog)*, 1869, oil on panel, 17 x 32.3 cm, Tom Thomson Art Gallery, Owen Sound, Ontario.

in nature, sometimes accompanied by Karl Friedrich Lessing (1808–1880).[19] As art historian Geraldine Norman notes, "[S]tudies made directly from nature were considered of the highest importance [for Biedermeier artists], though they were not normally sold per se but used as reference material for the composition of landscape paintings in the studio."[20]

Excursions into nature were valued for the sketches they produced, which were then used for later works painted in the studio. This practice was also shared by many other nineteenth-century European artists, including those associated with Romanticism (such as J.M.W. Turner [1775–1851]), the Barbizon School (including Jean-François Millet [1814–1875]), and Impressionism (including Claude Monet [1840–1926]). Raphael's penchant for *plein air* was reported by a journalist in the *Quebec Daily Mercury* in 1869: "He has made sketches of all the most remarkable points of this magnificent landscape [of Murray Bay]… and by the time of the next artists' exhibition, it is probable that some of these sketches will have recovered their vivid colors, their finish and their wonderfully picturesque contours."[21]

Like many of his predecessors and contemporaries, Raphael often used sketches as the basis for more finished works. In this way, different fragments of nature would influence the final composition. The Raphael painting that best evokes this process is

Fig 153 William Raphael, *An Amateur*, 1886, oil on canvas, 49.5 x 39.4 cm, collection of Jonathan Wener, Montreal.

Fig 154 William Raphael, *Man Seated*, 1882, graphite on wove paper, 18.9 x 12.1 cm, National Gallery of Canada, Ottawa.

An Amateur, 1886 (fig. 153).[22] The painting started with a few quick drawings in October 1882. On the sly, Raphael captured one of his students at work, palette in hand, seated on a portable three-legged stool (fig. 154).[23] This was probably Abbé Jules-Bernardin-Royal Rioux.[24] The scene, as we learn from an article in the *Gazette* in 1883, was also the subject of a pochade entitled *A Sketch from Nature* (fig. 50). The newspaper confirms what the title says: that this was a scene sketched on the spot. "[It] represents a reverend [curate] working at his easel unconscious of the companion artist behind; this represents an actual artist's excursion to Black River."[25] The pochade was exhibited at the Art Association of Montreal's salon in 1883. Two years later, Raphael reworked his composition into a more finely crafted version, altering the angle and size of the piece on the easel and adding the paintbox in the lower left of the work.[26] The finished painting, more detailed than the pochade, was then given the title *An Amateur* and shown at the 1886 spring exhibition.[27]

In both his drawings and his many sketches, Raphael was one of the first Canadian creators to carry out his artistic work directly outdoors, in the very landscapes he intended to paint. This *plein air* approach was a key element in the renewal of artistic practices in the nineteenth century, of which Raphael was one of the forerunners in Canada.

Sources & Resources

Zufriedenheit

I

Wie schön ist doch das ländliche Leben
Mein Häuschen steht auf grüner Flur
Von schattigen Bäumen umgeben.
Wie glücklich macht mich die Natur,
Im Schatten der blühenden Bäume
da sitz ich so gerne allein
Da reihen sich goldene Träume
der schönen Vergangenheit ein.

II

Zufrieden leb ich auf dem Lande
Obgleich ich kein Edelmann bin
Mir schwinden in mittlerem Stande
Die Tage so fröhlich dahin,

William Raphael's work, unlike that of contemporaries such as Cornelius Krieghoff, Napoléon Bourassa, and William Brymner, is not widely known. Beyond this book, only one in-depth study has been done to better define the artist and situate him historically—Sharon Goelman's master's thesis, submitted in 1978. Prior to its digitization, Goelman's thesis was restricted to the shelves of the Concordia University library. Although Goleman has since published two more texts on Raphael, his life, work, and legacy remain insufficiently studied within the discipline of Canadian art. The resources below are breadcrumbs to guide future scholars.

Key Exhibitions

The artist's environment and his professional associations and relationships are reflected by the exhibitions in which he participated during his lifetime. Interest in William Raphael's work waned in the final years in his life. After his death, his works were largely relegated to the background of Canadian art history, except for a few essential paintings. The first posthumous retrospective devoted to the artist was organized in 1996 at the Walter Klinkhoff Gallery in Montreal.

1859 **September:** Exhibition of *The Old Pedlar* at Dawson & Sons, Montreal.

1860 **August:** Presentation of an illuminated transparency in Jacques Cartier Square, Montreal.

1864 **February 11 to 13:** *Conversazione* and second loan exhibition, Art Association of Montreal.

1865 **February 27:** *Conversazione* and third loan exhibition, Art Association of Montreal.
September to October: Provincial Exhibition, Montreal.

1867 **February 5 to 16:** Fourth loan exhibition, Art Association of Montreal.

1868 **December 23:** First exhibition of the Society of Canadian Artists, Montreal.

1869 **March:** Exhibition of *Early Bird Picks Up the Worm* at Dawson & Sons, Montreal.
July: Exhibition of a Loch Achray landscape at Dawson & Sons, Montreal.

1870 **February 8 to 12:** Second exhibition of the Society of Canadian Artists, Montreal.
March 8 to 19: Sixth loan exhibition, Art Association of Montreal.

1879 **May 26 to September 26:** Ninth loan exhibition, Art Association of Montreal.
Exhibition, Ontario Society of Artists, Toronto.

1880 First annual exhibition, Canadian Academy of Arts (later the Royal Canadian Academy of Arts), Ottawa, Montreal, and Toronto.
First annual spring exhibition, Art Association of Montreal.

1881 **April 11 to 23:** Second annual spring exhibition, Art Association of Montreal.
July 5: Second annual exhibition, Canadian Academy of Art (later the Royal Canadian Academy of Arts), Halifax.

1882 **April 11 to May 3:** Third annual exhibition, Royal Canadian Academy of Arts, Montreal.

1883 **April 12 to 28:** Fourth annual spring exhibition, Art Association of Montreal.
May 23: Fourth annual exhibition, Royal Canadian Academy of Arts, Toronto.

William Raphael, manuscript of poem entitled *Das Ländliche Leben* (*Life in the Country*) (detail), July 6, 1851, National Gallery of Canada, Ottawa.

1884 **April 15 to May 4:** Fifth annual exhibition, Royal Canadian Academy of Arts, Montreal.

1885 **April 13 to May 2:** Sixth annual spring exhibition, Art Association of Montreal.
June: Exhibition of works by William Raphael's students at his studio, Montreal.

1886 **February 2:** Seventh annual exhibition, Royal Canadian Academy of Arts, Ottawa.
May 4 to October 15: Colonial and Indian Exhibition, London.

1887 **April 20:** Eighth annual exhibition, Royal Canadian Academy of Arts, Montreal.
June: Exhibition of works by William Raphael's students at his studio, Montreal.

1888 **April 3 to 21:** Ninth annual spring exhibition, Art Association of Montreal.

1889 **March 13:** Tenth annual exhibition, Royal Canadian Academy of Arts, Ottawa.
April 12 to May 4: Tenth annual spring exhibition, Art Association of Montreal.
June: Exhibition of works by William Raphael's students at his studio, Montreal.

1890 **April 24:** Eleventh annual exhibition, Royal Canadian Academy of Arts, Montreal.
May: Exhibition of a portrait at the store of framer W. H. Hope, Montreal.

1891 **March 6:** Twelfth annual exhibition, Royal Canadian Academy of Arts, Toronto.
April 20 to May 9: Twelfth annual spring exhibition, Art Association of Montreal.

1892 **March 30:** Thirteenth annual exhibition, Royal Canadian Academy of Arts, Ottawa.
April 18 to May 14: Thirteenth annual spring exhibition, Art Association of Montreal.

1893 **March 1:** Fourteenth annual exhibition, Royal Canadian Academy of Arts, Montreal.

1895 **March 6 to 30:** Sixteenth annual spring exhibition, Art Association of Montreal.
April 15: Sixteenth annual exhibition, Royal Canadian Academy of Arts, Toronto.
November: Exhibition in the artist's studio, Montreal.

1896 **March 12:** Seventeenth annual exhibition, Royal Canadian Academy of Arts, Montreal.

1898 **March 3:** Nineteenth annual exhibition, Royal Canadian Academy of Arts, Toronto.

1900 **March 16 to April 7:** Nineteenth annual spring exhibition, Art Association of Montreal.

1901 **March 8 to 23:** Twentieth annual spring exhibition, Art Association of Montreal.

Posthumous Exhibitions

1996 **September 7 to 21:** *William Raphael Retrospective*, Galerie Walter Klinkhoff, Montreal.

Journals Reviewing Raphael's Work

The Art Journal (London)
Canadian Illustrated News
Daily Witness
Evening Star
Evening Telegraph and Daily Commercial Advertiser
The Gazette (Montreal)
Hamilton Spectator
Le Journal de Québec
La Minerve
Montreal Herald and Daily Commercial Gazette
Montreal Star
Morning Chronicle and Commercial and Shipping Gazette
The New York Times
The Order
Ottawa Daily Citizen
Ottawa Journal
Le Pays
Le Progrès de l'Est: organ for the people of the Eastern Townships
Quebec Daily Mercury
Rose-Belford's Canadian Monthly and National Review
Toronto Star

Selected Critical Writings on Raphael

Béland, Mario. "Avant la dernière tempête." *Cap-aux-Diamants*, no. 53 (1998): 59.

Goelman, Sharon. "William Raphael, R.C.A. (1833–1914)." Master's thesis, Concordia University, 1978.

———. *William Raphael, R.C.A. (1833–1914)*. Montreal: Walter Klinkhoff Gallery, 1996. Exhibition catalogue.

———. "Raphael, William." *Dictionary of Canadian Biography*, vol. 14. Quebec and Toronto: Université Laval and University of Toronto, 1998.

Schachter, June. "William Osler and William Raphael." Osler Library, McGill University, *Osler Library Newsletter*, nos. 83–84 (1996–97): 1–3.

Selected Writings Referencing Raphael

Béland, Mario. "De Berczy à Krieghoff: Peintres étrangers au Bas-Canada 1790–1850." *Cap-aux-Diamants*, no. 37 (1994): 10–17.

———. "La muse hivernale: Fascination des artistes étrangers." *Cap-aux-Diamants*, no. 24 (1991): 50–54.

———. "Un peintre allemand à Montréal." *Cap-aux-Diamants*, no. 38 (1994): 65.

———, ed. *La peinture au Québec, 1820–1850, nouveaux regards, nouvelles perspectives*. Québec: Musée du Québec and Les publications du Québec, 1991.

Bouchard, Lydia. "Les paysages québécois de William Brymner, expérience de la nature comme lieu identitaire canadien au tournant du XXe siècle." Master's thesis, Université du Québec à Montréal, 2009.

Boulizon, Guy. *Le paysage dans la peinture au Québec*. Saint-Philippe-de-Laprairie: Éditions Marcel Broquet, 1984.

Boutilier, Alicia, and Paul Maréchal, eds. *William Brymner: Artist, Teacher, Colleague*. Kingston: Agnes Etherington Art Centre, Queen's University, 2010.

Cambron, Micheline. *Cultural Life in Montreal around 1900*. Montreal: Fides, 2005.

Cavell, Edward, and Dennis Reid. *When Winter Was King: The Image of Winter in 19th Century Canada*. Banff: Altitude Publishing, in association with the Whyte Museum of the Rockies, 1988.

Colgate, William. *Canadian Art: Its Origin and Development*. Toronto: McGraw-Hill Ryerson, 1967 (1943).

Dumas, Paul. "Pre-Contemporary Canadian Painting in the Collections of the Montreal Museum of Fine Arts." *Vie des arts* 20, no. 82 (1976): 31–35, 89–90.

Gavidia, Isolda. "Les théories ruskiennes de l'authenticité et leurs représentations dans les paysages nord-américains." Master's thesis, Université Laval, 2009.

Godsell, Patricia. *Enjoying Canadian Painting*. Toronto: General Publishing Co. Ltd., 1976.

Goldfarb, Hilliard T., ed. *Expanding Horizons: Painting and Photography of American and Canadian Landscape, 1860–1918*. Montreal: Montreal Museum of Fine Arts, 2009.

Grenier, Marlène. "Les artistes propagateurs de l'idéal allemand en art pictural et en sculpture au Canada au XIXe siècle." Master's thesis, Université Laval, 1996.

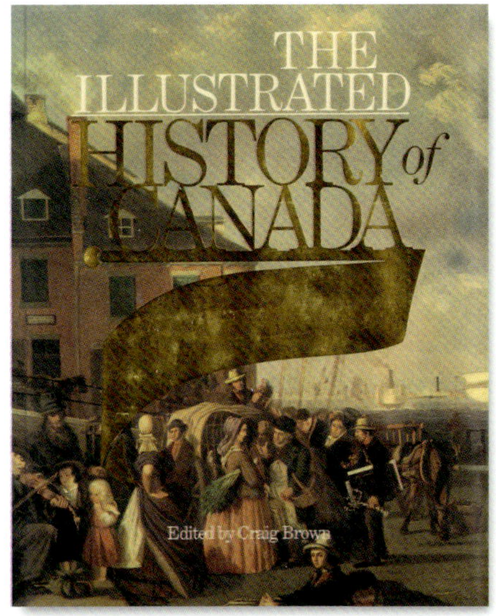

(LEFT) Cover of *The Illustrated History of Canada*, edited by Craig Brown (Lester & Orpen Dennys, 1987). (RIGHT) William Raphael, *The Walker*, 1870, oil on canvas, 58.4 x 44.5 cm, collection of Jonathan Wener, Montreal.

Gubbay, Aline. *A View of Their Own: The Story of Westmount*. Montreal: Price-Patterson Ltd., 1998.

Harper, John Russell. *Early Painters and Engravers in Canada*. Toronto: University of Toronto Press, 1970.

———. *Painting in Canada: A History*. Toronto: University of Toronto Press, 1966.

Hubbard, Robert Hamilton, ed. *An Anthology of Canadian Art*. Toronto: Oxford University Press, 1960.

Hubbard, Robert Hamilton, and Jean René Ostiguy. *Three Hundred Years of Canadian Art*. Ottawa: National Gallery of Canada, 1967.

Hubbard, Robert Hamilton, and Northrop Frye. *Canadian Landscape Painting 1670–1930: The Artist and the Land*. Madison: University of Wisconsin Press, 1973.

Ketner, Joseph D. *The Emergence of the African-American Artist: Robert S. Duncanson*. Columbia: University of Missouri Press, 1993.

Lacroix, Laurier. "La collection Maurice et Andrée Corbeil." *Vie des arts* 18, no. 72 (1973): 24–31.

———. "La construction picturale du Nord. La contribution des artistes canadiens au tournant du vingtième siècle." In *Couleurs et lumières du Nord*, edited by Maria Walecka-Garbalinska and Daniel Chartier. Stockholm: Acta Universitatis Stockholmiensis, 2008.

———. "Montreal and the Origins of the Canadian Academy of Arts." *Vie des arts* 24, no. 98 (1980): 20–23.

———. "Run Krieghoff cours." *Journal of Canadian Art History* 24 (2003): 60–71.
Lerner, Loren, and Mary F. Williamson. *Art and Architecture in Canada: A Bibliography and Guide to the Literature to 1981*. Toronto: University of Toronto Press, 1991, 2 volumes.
Lerner, Loren, and Suzanne Rackover. "Jews and Canadian Art." In *Canada's Jews: In Time, Space and Spirit*, edited by Ira Robinson. Brighton: Academic Studies Press, 2013.
Martin, Denis, and Michèle Grandbois. *La collection des dessins et estampes: 80 œuvres choisies*. Québec: Musée du Québec, 1991.
Montreal Museum of Fine Arts, *Quebec and Canadian Art*. Montreal: Montreal Museum of Fine Arts, 2011.
Morisset, Gérard. *La peinture traditionnelle au Canada français*. Ottawa: Le Cercle du livre de France (L'encyclopédie du Canada français, t. II), 1960.
Mulaire, Bernard. "Olindo Gratton et Louis-Philippe Hébert: Une relation professionnelle entre deux sculpteurs à la fin du XIXe siècle." *Journal of Canadian Art History* 12, no. 1 (1989): 22–49.
Nadeau-Saumier, Monique. "Un espace et un lieu de culture. Le *Art Building* de Sherbrooke 1887–1927." PhD dissertation, Université du Québec à Montréal, 2007.
Pearse, Harold. *From Drawing to Visual Culture: A History of Art Education*. Montreal and Kingston: McGill-Queen's University Press, 2006.
Poulter, Gillian. "Becoming Native in a Foreign Land: Visual Culture, Sport, and Spectacle in the Construction of National Identity in Montreal, 1840–1885." PhD dissertation, York University, 1999.
Ramsay, Ellen Louise. "The Promotion of the Fine Arts in Canada, 1880–1924: The Development of Art Patronage and the Formation of Public Policy." PhD dissertation, University College London, 1987.
Robert, Guy. *La peinture au Québec depuis ses origines*. Montréal: Québec Amérique, 1985 (1978).
Reid, Dennis. *A Concise History of Canadian Painting*. Toronto: Oxford University Press, 1988.
———. *Our Own Country Canada: Being an Account of the National Aspirations of the Principal Landscape Artists in Montreal and Toronto 1860–1890*. Ottawa: National Gallery of Canada and National Museums of Canada, 1979.
Robert, Guy. *La peinture au Québec depuis ses origines*. Montréal: Québec Amérique, 1985 (1978).
Sicotte, Hélène. "L'implantation de la galerie d'art à Montréal: Le cas de W. Scott & Sons, 1859–1914. Comment la révision du concept d'oeuvre d'art autorisa la spécialisation du commerce d'art." PhD dissertation, Université du Québec à Montréal, 2003.
Triggs, Stanley G. *William Notman: The Stamp of a Studio*. Toronto: Art Gallery of Ontario and Coach House Press, 1985.
Trudel, Jean. "L'Art Association of Montreal: Les années d'incertitude: 1863–1877." *Journal of Canadian Art History* 29 (2008): 116–45.
———. "Aux origines du Musée des beaux-arts de Montréal : la fondation de l'Art Association of Montréal en 1860," 15, no. 1 (1992): 31–62.
———. "Une élite et son musée." *Cap-au-Diamants*, no. 25 (1991): 22–25.
Vallée, Anne-Élisabeth. "La contribution artistique, pédagogique et théorique de Napoléon Bourassa à la vie culturelle montréalaise entre 1855 et 1890." PhD dissertation, Université du Québec à Montréal, 2009.
———. *Napoléon Bourassa et la vie culturelle à Montréal au XIXe siècle*. Montreal: Leméac, 2010.

Further Reading

Bell, Duncan. *The Idea of Greater Britain: Empire and the Future of World Order, 1860–1900*. Princeton: Princeton University Press, 2011.
Brown, Michael. "The American Connection of Canadian Jews: 1759–1914." *AJS Review* 3 (1978): 21–77.
Cohen, Naomi W. "American Jewish Reactions to Anti-Semitism in Western Europe, 1875–1900." *Proceedings of the American Academy for Jewish Research* 45 (1978): 29–65.
———. "Early Zionism in Canada and the United States." *Jewish Social Studies* 44, no. 2 (Spring 1982): 149–68.
———. *Jew or Juif? Jews, French Canadians, and Anglo-Canadians: 1759–1914*. Philadelphia: Jewish Publication Society of America, 1986.
Feldman, David. "Jews and the British Empire c.1900." *History Workshop Journal*, no. 63 (2007): 70-89.
Horsman, Reginald. "Origins of Racial Anglo-Saxonism in Great Britain before 1850." *Journal of the History of Ideas* 37, no. 3 (1976): 387–410.
Kaufmann, Eric P. *The Rise and Fall of Anglo-America*. Cambridge: Harvard University Press, 2004.
Lessard, Michel. *La nouvelle encyclopédie des antiquités du Québec*. Montreal: Les Éditions de l'Homme, 2007.
Mendelson, Alan. *Exiles from Nowhere: The Jews and the Canadian Elite*. Montreal: Robin Brass Studio.
Neumann-Schliski, Jens. "Un programme commun? Conceptions de l'identité juive dans les Archives israélites et l'Allgemeine Zeitung des Judenthums, 1840–1881." In *Expériences croisées: Juifs de France et d'Allemagne aux XIXe et XXe siècles*, edited by Heidi Knörzer. Paris: Éditions de l'éclat, 2010.
Pearce, Lisa D., and Claire C. Gilliland. *Religion in America*. Berkeley: University of California Press, 2020.
Wagner, Jonathan. *A History of Migration from Germany to Canada, 1850–1939*. Vancouver: UBC Press, 2006.

A Familial Connection

Jonathan Wener, William Raphael's great-great-grandson, has championed his ancestor's legacy. By collecting, restoring, and sharing Raphael's works, he has built an essential reference collection. His mission is to bring renewed visibility to this underacknowledged Canadian painter.

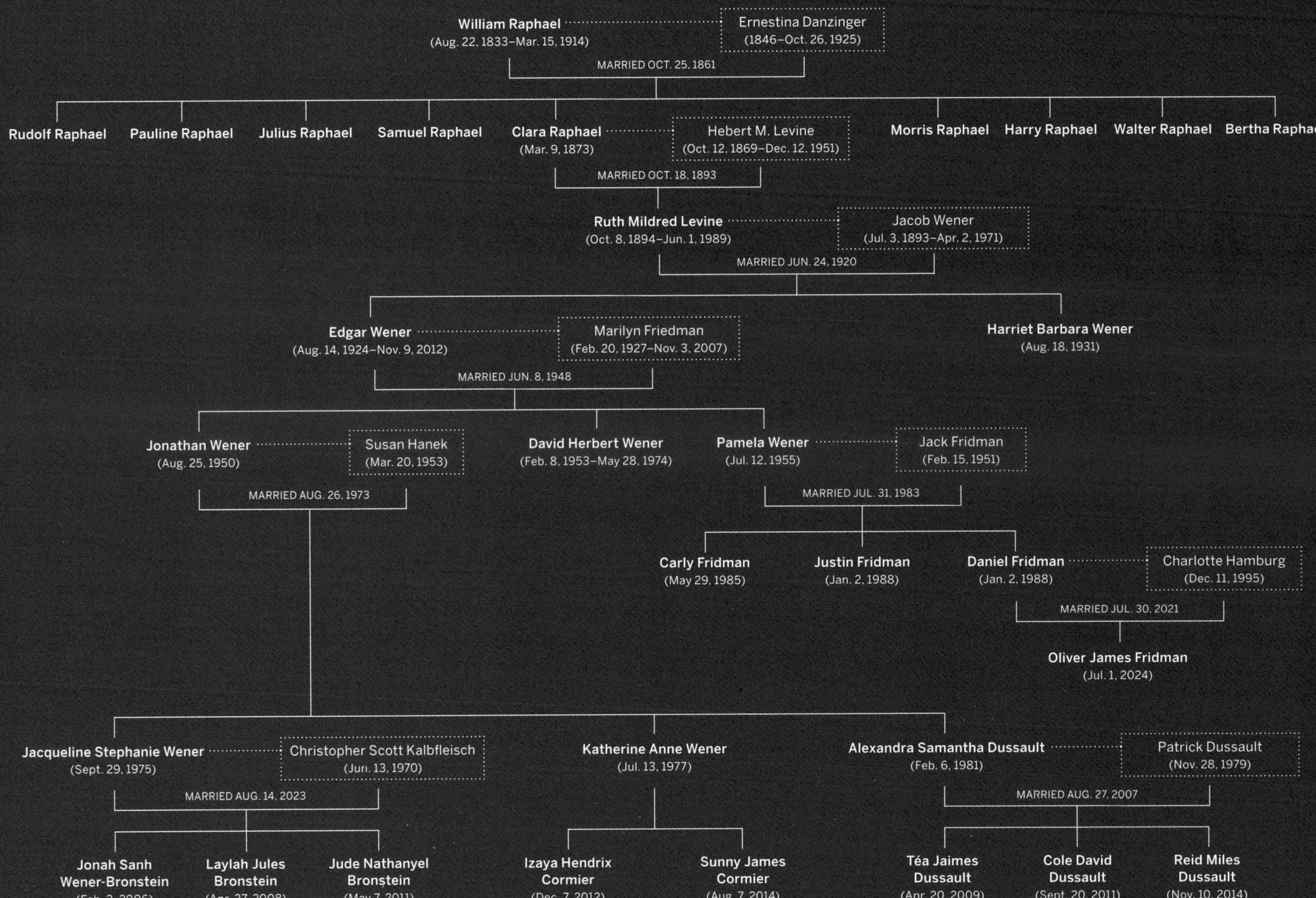

Notes

BIOGRAPHY

1 As evidenced by two sketchbooks preserved at the McCord Stewart Museum in Montreal. Sharon Goelman, "William Raphael, R.C.A. (1833–1914)" (master's thesis, Concordia University, 1978), 10. Goelman's pioneering work on the artist's life and career brought to light many relevant sources that have aided in constructing his rich biography. I am indebted to her many discoveries, some of which have been published, notably in Sharon Goelman, *William Raphael, R.C.A. (1833–1914)*, exh. cat. (Galerie Walter Klinkhoff, 1996), and in Sharon Goelman, "Raphael, William," in *Dictionary of Canadian Biography*, vol. 14 (University of Toronto / Université Laval, 1998), https://www.biographi.ca/en/bio/raphael_william_14E.html.

2 Goelman, "William Raphael," 13–14.

3 Goelman, "William Raphael," 14–17.

4 Goelman, "William Raphael," 12, 18–19.

5 Ulrike Möhlenbeck, head of the historical archives at the Academy of Arts in Berlin, explained: "Among the 28,000 names of students, I have unfortunately been unable to find any reference to William Raphael (Raffaelsky). Our records are not complete, as some of the student lists were lost during the Second World War." Ulrike Möhlenbeck, email message to author, September 14, 2023. This same observation was made by Sharon Goelman, "William Raphael," 257–58nn56–57.

6 Goelman, "William Raphael," 19.

7 Raphael may also have had lessons with Begas, as he claimed in 1886, since Begas did indeed teach composition and drapery at the Royal Academy in Berlin from 1829 to 1854. Goelman, "William Raphael," 257–58n56. In 1853, did indeed teach a composition course. "Minutes of the Academic Senate and Plenary Assemblies of 1853 and 1854," April 17, 1853, 03.2. Protokolle der Sitzungen des Senats, der Mitglieder und der Gesamtakademie, PrAdK 049, Akademie Der Künste Archiv, Berlin. Initially a Nazarene, Begas changed his practice in the 1840s to embrace genre scenes and adopt a realistic approach in the spirit of Biedermeier. Eberhard Ruhmer, "Begas, Karl the Elder," *Neue Deutsche Biographie*, vol. 1, 1953, 744–45.

8 Herbig mainly taught drawing. In 1850, he was appointed acting director of the academy, a position he held until 1861. "Friedrich Wilhelm Heinrich Herbig," Akademie Der Künste, https://www.adk.de/de/akademie/mitglieder/index.htm?we_objectID=54629.

9 Despite the desire for reform in the first half of the nineteenth century, the academic system in Berlin remained linked to the models already in place in Italy and France. Hans Gerhard Hannesen, *Die Akademie der Künste in Berlin: Facetten einer 300jährigen Geschichte* (Berlin: Akademie der Künste, 2005), 10–11, 111–18.

10 A professor of anatomical drawing taught at the academy. Students were even allowed to draw from cadavers, under the guidance of their teacher. Johann Friedrich Unger, ed., *Reglement für die Akademie der bildenden Künste und mechanischen Wissenschaften zu Berlin* (Berlin, 1790), 20.

11 Goelman, "William Raphael," 8–9.

12 Jonathan Wagner, *A History of Migration from Germany to Canada*, 1850–1939 (UBC Press, 2006), 22–23.

13 See the numerous drawings in William Raphael's "Sketchbook No. 2," in the National Gallery of Canada, Ottawa. Goelman, "William Raphael," 32–33.

14 Arthur J. Maginnis, *The Atlantic Ferry: Its Ships, Men, and Working* (Whittaker & Co., 1893), 95. The *Borussia* was designed in 1855 by the Hamburg-American Line and made its maiden voyage on June 1, 1856.

15 "The Hamburg steamship *Borussia*," *Daily National Intelligencer*, December 24, 1856, 1.

16 "The Hamburg steamship *Borussia*," 1.

17 Despite William Raphael's drawings and notes, which prove that he made the crossing on the *Borussia* in December 1856, the list of the ship's 279 passengers, compiled in New York, does not include his name (or the variants Israel Rafalsky or Raphaelsky). "List or Manifest of All the Passengers On Board the Steamship *Borussia*, December 22, 1856 (November 18 to December 31, 1856)," *Passenger Lists of Vessels Arriving at New York*, 1820–1897 (Washington: National Archives Microfilm Publications, 1958), microform, 169.

18 Goelman, "William Raphael," 38–39.

19 "Sketchbook No. 3," National Gallery of Canada, Ottawa. Goelman, "William Raphael," 39–40.

20 As recorded by the artist in his "Sketchbook" from the Collection of Jonathan Wener, Montreal. Goelman, "William Raphael," 39.

21 Laurier Lacroix and Suzanne Sauvage, eds., *James Duncan (1806–1881): Painter of Montreal* (Montreal: McCord Stewart Museum, 2023). See especially the chapter "Discovering Duncan" by Laurier Lacroix, 12–45. Apart from Duncan, *Mackay's Montreal Directory, for 1856–57* lists only two other Montreal-based artists, about which there is very little information: painter John Hawksett and a certain Robert Parker, 125, 218.

22 "Sketchbook No. 3," Goelman, "William Raphael," 41.

23 Arlene Gehmacher, *Paul Kane: Life & Work* (Toronto: Art Canada Institute, 2014), 5, 13–14.

24 The artist lists the portraits made during this period in "Sketchbook No. 3." Goelman, "William Raphael," 41–42.

25 *Mackay's Montreal Directory, for 1856–57*, 317.

26 "Photography: W. Notman," *Montreal Herald and Daily Commercial Gazette*, March 2, 1859, 1.

27 "Sketchbook No. 5." Goelman, "William Raphael," 82–83, 276n101. Similarly, in the article "Fine Arts" (*Montreal Herald and Daily Commercial Gazette*, September 30, 1859, 2), William Raphael is associated with William Notman's studio.

28 From "Oil Painted Photographs," *Morning Chronicle* (Quebec), December 17, 1859, 2. The portrait could not be traced.

29 "The Prince's Arrival," *Montreal Herald and Daily Commercial Gazette*, August 27, 1860, supplement, 2.

30 In particular, there is a portrait of a woman preserved at the McCord Stewart Museum. William Raphael, after William Notman, *Unidentified Lady, Painted Photograph, Montreal*, 1860, oil and silver salts on paper mounted on canvas, 50.8 x 40.6 cm, McCord Stewart Museum (N-1978.1.1). This painting on photograph is signed and dated 1860. A portrait of a man, inscribed "W. Notman / W.R. / Montreal / 1860," is also reported by Goelman but its current location remains unknown. Goelman, "William Raphael," 83–84.

31 William Raphael, "The Art Gallery," *The Gazette* (Montreal), June 18, 1886, 5.

William Raphael, *The Coachman* (detail), c.1860–1900, collection of Jonathan Wener, Montreal.

32 Further research into the Dawson family's role would be welcome. A quick glance at a few newspapers of the period highlights their activity in the Montreal art scene. See, for example, "Paintings on Exhibition," *Montreal Herald and Daily Commercial Gazette*, March 5, 1857, 3; "A Sculptor," *The Gazette* (Montreal), June 7, 1859, 2; "Photography on a Large Scale," *Montreal Herald and Daily Commercial Gazette*, May 3, 1860, 2; "The Royal Family," *Montreal Herald and Daily Commercial Gazette*, August 27, 1860, 1. See also George L. Parker, "Dawson, Samuel Edward," in *Dictionary of Canadian Biography*, vol. 14 (University of Toronto / Université Laval, 1998), 301–303, https://www.biographi.ca/en/bio/dawson_samuel_edward_14E.html.

33 "Fine Arts," *Montreal Herald*, 2.

34 "Fine Arts," *Montreal Herald*, 2.

35 "Oil Painted Photographs," *Morning Chronicle* (Quebec), 2. Long referred to as the "Man with the Hat," the portrait has the features of a young William Raphael, as photographed in 1862 by Notman (with a very similar hat in his hand).

36 "The Prince's Arrival," *Montreal Herald*, 2.

37 Mario Béland, "Un peintre allemand à Montréal," *Cap-aux-Diamants*, no. 38 (Summer 1994): 65.

38 Jean-Claude Robert, "Urbanisation et population: Le cas de Montréal en 1861," *Revue d'histoire de l'Amérique française* 35, no. 4 (1982): 523–24.

39 Jean Trudel, "Aux origines du Musée des beaux-arts de Montréal: La fondation de l'Art Association of Montreal en 1860," *Journal of Canadian Art History / Annales d'histoire de l'art Canadien* 15, no. 1 (1992): 38.

40 Jean Trudel, "Une élite et son musée," *Cap-aux-Diamants*, no. 25 (1991): 23.

41 Trudel, "Aux origines du Musée des beaux-arts de Montréal," 43–44.

42 Generally held in the exhibition space, a *conversazione* is enlivened by speeches and music, and guests are invited to take part in the various discussions. Jean Trudel, "Art Association of Montreal: Les années d'incertitude, 1863–1877," *Journal of Canadian Art History / Annales d'histoire de l'art Canadien 29* (2008): 125. See also Anne-Élisabeth Vallée, *Napoléon Bourassa et la vie culturelle à Montréal au XIXe siècle* (Montreal: Leméac, 2010), 49.

43 Goelman, "William Raphael," 41, 266n182.

44 William Raphael occasionally borrows money from Mr. Danziger. Goelman, "William Raphael," 44.

45 "Census of 1861, Canada East, district no. 38 Montreal, sub-district no. 14 Montreal (Saint-Louis-de-France)," 1861, RG31—Statistics Canada, microfilm C-1245, image 4108553_01219, Library and Archives Canada, Ottawa, http://central.bac-lac.gc.ca/.redirect?app=census&id=44272157&lang=eng. Goelman, "William Raphael," 44, 267n202.

46 Goelman, "William Raphael," 44.

47 "Engagement de William Raphael à Abner Bedee Taber," January 15, 1863, no. 8203, Joseph-E.-Odilon Labadie registry, Bibliothèque et Archives nationales du Québec, Montreal.

48 *Mackay's Montreal Directory, for 1863–1864*, (J. Lovell, 1863), 286.

49 "Engagement de William Raphael à Abner Bedee Taber."

50 The term "speculative" is used to describe works that are not direct commissions. In other words, the artist produces his paintings without any guarantee of payment and then releases them to the market in the hope that a buyer will eventually be interested in acquiring them. For this notion of speculative production, see John Michael Montias, *Le marché de l'art aux Pays-Bas* (Paris: Flammarion, 1996), 33–37.

51 "The Fine Art Conversazione: Second Notice," *The Gazette* (Montreal), February 13, 1864, 2. See also Hélène Sicotte, "L'implantation de la galerie d'art à Montréal: Le cas de W. Scott & Sons, 1859–1914. Comment la révision du concept d'oeuvre d'art autorisa la spécialisation du commerce d'art" (PhD diss., Université du Québec à Montréal, 2003), 246–47.

52 Trudel, "Art Association of Montreal," 125–27.

53 Quoted in Goelman, "William Raphael," 124, and in Trudel, "Art Association of Montreal," 127.

54 "Exhibition [...] Art Association," *Evening Telegraph and Daily Commercial Advertiser*, March 1, 1865, 4. At the third Art Association of Montreal exhibition, held in 1865, a reviewer noted: "Another Canadian artist (Raphael), not unknown to fame, perhaps one of the most thoroughly educated historical painters in Canada, we see slightly represented. His *Dog and Sleigh* is however a spirited little group, *though we might have expected a second great work of local, interest like that of his Bonsecours Market which did such credit to Canadian art in our first Exhibition*" (emphasis added).

55 Goelman, "William Raphael," 44–45.

56 "Exhibition [...] Art Association," 4.

57 "Art Notes," *The Gazette* (Montreal), July 10, 1869, 1.

58 *Mackay's Montreal Directory, for 1865–66* (J. Lovell, 1865), 257. Goelman, "William Raphael", 45. Suzanne LaFerrière, "Les visages du Plateau Mont-Royal," *Continuité*, no. 66 (Fall 1995): 15.

59 In 1866, the Raphaels moved to 303 German Street, and the following year, they moved to 302 German Street. *Mackay's Montreal Directory, for 1866-67* (J. Lovell, 1866), 268; *Mackay's Montreal Directory, for 1867-68* (J. Lovell, 1867), 271. German Street is now a section of Avenue de Hôtel-de-Ville.

60 "Provincial Exhibition," *Montreal Herald and Daily Commercial Gazette*, September 30, 1865, 2; "Liste des prix à l'Exhibition provinciale," *Le pays*, October 5, 1865, 2.

61 Allan Pringle, "Robert S. Duncanson in Montreal, 1863–1865," *The American Art Journal* 17, no. 4 (Autumn 1985): 30–33.

62 "Art in Continental States," *The Art Journal*, November 1, 1866, 330: "[T]he same artist has just completed another picture, entitled 'The Fortune Teller.' It carries us back to 'long, long ago;' and sets us down in a wood situated near an old castle, a glimpse of which may be had through the trees. In the foreground is an elderly man and his family, who are having the future unveiled to them by a gipsy fortune-teller, several of whose companions, in a variety of attitudes, are standing around. The picture displays considerable genius, and speaks well for the artist."

63 *Mackay's Montreal Directory, for 1866–67*, 268.

64 This vision of the benefits of artistic practice was supported by, for example, painter Napoléon Bourassa, when he wanted to set up drawing classes in Montreal in the early 1860s. See Anne-Élisabeth Vallée, "La contribution artistique, pédagogique et théorique de Napoléon Bourassa à la vie culturelle montréalaise entre 1855 et 1890" (PhD diss., Université du Québec à Montréal, 2009), 115–17.

65 The artist relocated his studio to 67 rue Saint James in 1867 and then to 171 rue Saint James in 1870. Between 1871 and 1873, his studio was located at 12 Place d'Armes. In 1875, Raphael announced that his studio was now located at 217 rue Saint James.

66 As shown in the city directories edited by Lovell and published between 1878 and 1883.

67 William Raphael does not appear to have been a founding member. The list of members, as printed in the Society of Canadian Artists' first catalogue (published in 1868), does not mention Raphael by name, despite his participation in the exhibition. See Society of Canadian Artists,

First Exhibition 1868: Catalogue of Oil and Water Colour Paintings, Statuary, &c., Exhibited at the Gallery of the Art Association, at the Mercantile Library Building, Montreal, 23rd December, 1868 (Montreal: n.p., 1868).

68 "Chromo Lithographic Art," *Evening Star* (Montreal), October 12, 1870, 2.

69 Trudel, "Art Association of Montreal," 127.

70 "The Fine Arts," *Quebec Daily Mercury*, August 20, 1869, 2.

71 Gaëtan Gervais, "Le commerce de détail au Canada (1870–1888)," *Revue d'histoire de l'Amérique française* 33, no. 4 (1980): 548.

72 This relationship was established in a text prepared by the Pointe-à-Callière Museum and published online. See "Portraits," Pointe-à-Callière Museum, https://collections.pacmusee.qc.ca/en/objects/portrait-2018-001-001/.

73 June Schachter, "William Osler and William Raphael," Osler Library, McGill University, *Osler Library Newsletter*, nos. 83–84 (1996–97), 1–3.

74 In 1912, the Art Association of Montreal moved into a new building at 1380 Sherbrooke Street West. In 1948–49, the AAM changed its name to the Montreal Museum of Fine Arts. Trudel, "Aux origines du Musée des beaux-arts de Montréal," 31.

75 "The New Art Gallery," *The Gazette* (Montreal), May 27, 1879, 2; Georges-Hébert Germain, *A City's Museum: A History of the Montreal Museum of Fine Arts* (Montreal: Montreal Museum of Fine Arts, 2007), 2.

76 Art Association of Montreal, *Ninth Exhibition 1879: Catalogue of Oil and Water Colour Paintings, Exhibited by the Association on the Occasion of the Opening of the Art Gallery, Phillips' Square May 26th, 1879* (Art Association of Montreal, 1879), 145.

77 Goelman, "William Raphael," 58.

78 Goelman, "William Raphael," 59. The other three paintings were *Pointe-au-Pic, Murray Bay*; *Tandem*; and *Habitant* (or *Preparing to Smoke*).

79 "Toronto," *Hamilton Spectator*, September 13, 1879, 1.

80 "Fine Arts," *Ottawa Daily Citizen*, September 23, 1879, 1.

81 "Ex Parte on the Application of William Raphael for Naturalization, Filed 22 August 1872," Citizenship Registration, Montreal Circuit Court, 1851 to 1945, RG 6 F3, volume 901, file 58, Library and Archives Canada, Ottawa, https://recherche-collection-search.bac-lac.gc.ca/eng/Home/Record?app=citregmtlcircou&IdNumber=2723&q_type_1=q&q_1=William%20Raphael&ecopy=vol901-00000058-00000001.

82 Goelman, "William Raphael," 59.

83 Jim Burant, *Ottawa Art & Artists: An Illustrated History* (Toronto: Art Canada Institute, 2022), 135.

84 "Ottawa—Opening of the Canadian Academy of Arts by His Excellency the Gov.-General," *Hamilton Spectator*, March 11, 1880, 3.

85 Goelman, "William Raphael," 60.

86 The other three works were by Marmaduke Matthews, Henry Sandham, and Thomas M. Martin.

87 "The Pictures of the Week," *Canadian Illustrated News*, April 10, 1880, 226.

88 "Personal," *Hamilton Spectator*, March 8, 1880, 4.

89 "A Gossip About the First Dominion Art Exhibition by an Unlearned Visitor," *Rose-Belford's Canadian Monthly and National Review* 4 (January–June 1880), 552. The journalist noted two paintings by Raphael depicting a habitant. Strangely, the article states that "Mr. Gilmour, to whom they were sold, is to be congratulated on their acquisition." Since the newspapers had reported that the *Habitant* work was acquired by the Marquess of Lorne, the author of the article is probably mistaken. Perhaps the second work was actually acquired by this Mr. Gilmour.

90 Goelman, "William Raphael," 58–69.

91 Goelman, "William Raphael," 62.

92 Goelman, "William Raphael," 90–91.

93 Throughout his career, William Raphael produced only a handful of religious paintings, including *Sainte Famille* (Maison Saint-Gabriel) in 1882; *Le Purgatoire visité par la Vierge* (Sisters of Sainte-Anne) in 1894; two pendants, each depicting an angel, for the chapel of the Sisters of Sainte-Anne (Musée de Lachine), in 1897; and a representation of the Virgin for the Congrégation de Notre-Dame, around 1909. Similarly, a painting of the Annunciation can be seen behind the artist in a photograph showing Raphael in his studio, c.1890. See details in the image opening the biography section (p. 8). Goelman, "William Raphael," 98–99, 184–87.

94 "Art Education," *The Gazette* (Montreal), December 11, 1880, 3.

95 "Art Education," *The Gazette* (Montreal).

96 "Art Education," *The Gazette* (Montreal).

97 According to a note preserved at the McCord Stewart Museum, Dr. J.H. Jacobs identified this chief as A-wen-na-ni-io, grandfather of Sa-ron-he-se Deer and Madame Joseph D'Ailleboust.

98 "Picturesque Canada," *The Gazette* (Montreal), May 10, 1882, 5. The article praises the "wonderfully natural" aspect of William Raphael's work.

99 Michel Dreyfus, "Durant l'affaire Dreyfus (1894–1906)," in *L'antisémitisme à gauche: Histoire d'un paradoxe, de 1830 à nos jours* (Paris: La Découverte, 2011), 69–97.

100 Isaac Besht Bendavid, "Goldwin Smith and the Jews," *North American Review* 153, no. 418 (1891): 259.

101 Alan Mendelson, "*Grip* Magazine and 'the Other': The Genteel Antisemitism of J.W. Bengough," *Histoire sociale / Social History* 40, no. 79 (2007), 1–44.

102 Michael Brown, "From Stereotype to Scapegoat: Anti-Jewish Sentiment in French Canada from Confederation to World War I," in *Jew or Juif? Jews, French Canadians, and Anglo-Canadians: 1759–1914* (Philadelphia: Jewish Publication Society, 1986), 55.

103 Alan Mendelson, *Exiles from Nowhere: The Jews and the Canadian Elite* (Montreal: Robin Brass Studio, 2008), 11–13.

104 "Art Association of Montreal, Council Meetings," September 6, 1882, Archives of the Montreal Museum of Fine Arts, Montreal.

105 From the earliest years of the South Kensington Museum's educational program in the mid-nineteenth century, the institution was a model to follow in the British colony. In Canada West (Ontario), it was supported by educator Egerton Ryerson (1803–1882), who emphasized its value in various publications. See Ellen Louise Ramsay, "The Promotion of the Fine Arts in Canada, 1880–1924: The Development of Art Patronage and the Formation of Public Policy" (PhD diss., University College London, 1987), 36.

106 "The Art Exhibition," *The Gazette* (Montreal), April 16, 1883, 3.

107 Brymner offered the first course of this kind in 1889 at the Art Association of Montreal. See Jocelyn Anderson, *William Brymner: Life & Work* (Toronto: Art Canada Institute, 2020), 14.

108 "Montreal Society of Decorative Art," *Montreal Star*, October 17, 1881, 2; "Montreal Society of Decorative Art," *The Gazette* (Montreal), May 28, 1883, 3; "Decorative Art," *The Gazette* (Montreal), May 27, 1884, 3.

109 "Mrs. Lovell's Young Ladies Institute," *Montreal Star*, June 13, 1884, 3.

110 Goelman, "William Raphael," 63–64.

111 *Lovell's Montreal Directory, for 1884–85* (Lovell, 1884), 563.

112 "W. Raphael's Classes," *Montreal Star*, September 16, 1884, 1. The ad was repeated on September 18, 22, 23, and 29, as well as on October 2, 6, 9, and 11.

113 The last ad appeared in the *Montreal Star* on September 26, 1908.

114 "Exhibition of Drawings," *Montreal Star*, June 6, 1885, 8.

115 "The Art Exhibition," *The Gazette* (Montreal), June 9, 1885, 3.

116 "Our Artists at Work," *Montreal Star*, March 14, 1885, 2.

117 Anderson, *William Brymner: Life & Work*, 13–14.

118 "The Royal Canadian Academy," *Montreal Star*, February 22, 1886, 2; "Montreal's Art Gallery," *The Gazette* (Montreal), June 3, 1886, 7.

119 "The Art Gallery," *The Gazette* (Montreal), June 5, 1886, 4.

120 "The Art Gallery," *The Gazette* (Montreal), June 18, 1886, 5.

121 Anderson, *William Brymner: Life & Work*, 7.

122 Hélène Sicotte, "William Brymner: A Remarkably Sociable Man," in *William Brymner: Artist, Teacher, Colleague*, eds. Alicia Boutilier and Paul Maréchal (Kingston, ON: Agnes Etherington Art Centre, Queen's University, 2010), 23.

123 See, in particular, a lecture from 1895 in which Brymner develops a point about bad chromolithographs, which seems to be directed at Raphael, who was recognized for his success translating his works into this medium. Moreover, Brymner discusses the detestable use of these images for educational purposes, through copying. He says: "Copies of meritless or good chromo-lithographs teach nothing, lead to nothing and to worse than nothing." It is worth noting that four years earlier, one of Raphael's students, a Mrs. Pinkerton, had earned praise for her copy of the painting *The Angelus* by Jean-François Millet (1814–1875), which was probably produced with the help of an image. "Mr. Brymner on Drawing," *Montreal Star*, March 28, 1895, 5; "The Angelus," *Montreal Star*, September 11, 1891, 4.

124 Goelman, "William Raphael," 79–80.

125 Goelman, "William Raphael," 64–69.

126 "The Picture Market," *Daily Witness*, March 14, 1888, 5.

127 Monique Nadeau-Saumier, "Un espace et un lieu de culture. Le Art Building de Sherbrooke 1887–1927 (PhD diss., Université du Québec à Montréal, 2007), 317–19.

128 Contrary to what has been suggested in the literature (see Goelman, "William Raphael," 81), Raphael was never a teacher at the Conseil des arts et des manufactures. This institution actually hired the dealer Henry William Raphael in 1904. See "In and Around the City," *Montreal Star*, May 24, 1904, 11.

129 As quoted in Goelman, "William Raphael," 100.

130 Goelman, "William Raphael," 121.

131 "Montreal Artist Dead—Mr. William Raphael Was 81 Years Old," *The Gazette* (Montreal), March 16, 1914, 8; "Wm. Raphael, Artist, Dead," *Montreal Star*, March 16, 1914, 2; "Wm. Raphael Dead," *Toronto Star*, March 16, 1914, 4; "William Raphael," *American Art News* 12, no. 24 (March 21, 1914), 4.

KEY WORKS

HAYMARKET SQUARE / VICTORIA SQUARE

1 Laurier Lacroix produced a study of this work for the Klinkhoff gallery. This section of the text is based on that study. As the author points out, the first market was established in 1810 by curators James McGill, Jon Richardson, and Jean-Marie Mondelet. This was the Place des Commissaires. In 1841, this area was turned into a park, and an adjoining site was purchased for use as a commercial space called Beaver Square. Beaver Square became Victoria Square in 1860. The hay market remained in operation here until it was relocated to a larger space in 1865.

2 Jonathan Cha, "Formes et sens des squares victoriens montréalais dans le contexte de développement de la métropole (1801–1914)" (PhD diss., Université du Québec à Montréal / Université Paris-Est, 2013), 103–107.

3 Guy Pinard, *Montréal: Son histoire, son architecture* (Montreal: La Presse, 1987), 192–93.

4 Karim Wagih Fawzi Youssef, "Le développement morphologique du Square Victoria à Montréal" (master's thesis, Université de Montréal, 2002), 28.

BEHIND BONSECOURS MARKET, MONTREAL

1 "Exposition provinciale," *Journal de Québec*, September 27, 1865, 2.

2 "Exposition provinciale," *Journal de Québec*, 2.

3 "L'exposition," *La Minerve*, September 27, 1865, 2.

4 See, in particular, Napoléon Bourassa, *Influence du sentiment religieux sur l'art*, unpublished manuscript, n.d., Library and Archives Canada, Fonds Napoléon-Bourassa (R7636-0-3-F). This manuscript was reproduced as an appendix to Anne-Élisabeth Vallée, "La contribution artistique, pédagogique et théorique de Napoléon Bourassa à la vie culturelle montréalaise entre 1855 et 1890" (PhD diss., Université du Québec à Montréal, 2009), 505–30.

5 Napoléon Bourassa, "Causerie artistique sur l'exposition de l'Art Association," *La Revue Canadienne* 2, no. 3 (March 1865): 171.

6 "Provincial Exhibition," *Montreal Herald and Daily Commercial Gazette*, September 30, 1865, 2.

7 "Art in Continental States," *The Art Journal*, October 1, 1866, 306.

8 "Art in Continental States," *The Art Journal*, November 1, 1866, 330.

9 Dennis Reid, *Our Own Country Canada: Being an Account of the National Aspirations of Principal Landscape Artists in Montreal and Toronto 1860–1890* (Ottawa: National Gallery of Canada / National Museums of Canada, 1979), 88.

10 Reid, *Our Own Country Canada*, 89. Reid suggests that the figure at the centre of the composition, holding a portfolio, could be the artist. The idea is taken up by David Burnett in *Masterpieces of Canadian Art from the National Gallery of Canada* (Edmonton: Hurtig Publishers, 1990). When this work is compared with photographic portraits of William Raphael, however, there does not appear to be any clear resemblance to the painter.

THE EARLY BIRD PICKS UP THE WORM

1 A critic of the *Gazette* described the image as follows: "A successful beggar emerges from a door, where he meets a lazier comrade who arrives too late." See "Society of Canadian Artists," 2.

2 "Chromo Lithography," *Daily Witness*, 4, March 13, 1869.

3 "La Chromo-Lithographie en Canada," *Le Pays*, March 15, 1869, 2. Also of note is a highly complimentary article in the *Montreal Herald* that also credits Reinhold: "Chromo Lithography," *Montreal Herald and Daily Commercial Gazette*, March 8, 1869, 2.

4 "Chromo Lithography," *Daily Witness*, 4.

5 They won first prize for lithographic drawings at the Montreal Provincial Exhibition in 1865. See "Provincial Exhibition," *Montreal Herald and Daily Commercial Gazette*, September 30, 1865, 2.

6 In fact, according to the newspaper *Le Pays*, chromolithography "required the use of fifteen or twenty lithographic stones" to reproduce Raphael's work in colour in a number of stages. "La Chromo-Lithographie en Canada," 2.

7 "No other such set is known to exist," says Canadian engraving specialist Rosemarie L. Tovell. See National Gallery of Canada Archives, work file no. 37168.1-21, acquisition justification signed by Rosemarie L. Tovell, November 1993. Moreover, as the expert also points out, the series of prints in the National Gallery of Canada's collection is believed to have come from the personal estates of Reinhold or Roberts.

TANDEM

1 "Artistic," *Evening Star* (Montreal), January 29, 1869, 2.

2 Mario Béland, "Avant la dernière tempête," *Cap-aux-Diamants*, no. 53 (1998): 59.

3 Will H. Whyte, "Sleighing," *Outing* 13, no. 5 (February 1889): 387–91; Lucinda M. Fisher, "Montreal Sleighing Memories," *Carriage Journal* 27, no. 3 (Winter 1989): 107–11

4 The 1878 work was exhibited at the 1879 Ontario Society of Artists show in Toronto. Sharon Goelman, "William Raphael, R.C.A. (1833–1914)" (master's thesis, Concordia University, 1978), 59.

THE MCFARLANE CHILDREN

1 Mario Béland, "Théophile Hamel et les portraits d'enfants," *Cap-aux-Diamants*, no. 143 (Fall 2020): 57–59.

2 Two other works signed by Inglis and Raphael, dated 1872, are kept in the collection of the Musée d'art de Joliette. They are portraits of an unidentified couple, presented as pendants.

3 See a study of the painting by Victoria A. Baker, dated August 19, 1987. This acquisition record is kept in the work file at the National Gallery of Canada (29786).

HABITANT (OR PREPARING TO SMOKE)

1 Based on the 1881 Canadian census, this could be Jean-Baptiste Sarrasin, a farmer residing in Saint-Didace, in the Maskinongé district. "Census of 1881, Quebec, district no. 85 Maskinongé, sub-district Saint-Didace (J)," 1881, RG31—Statistics Canada, microfilm C-13214, image e008157833, Library and Archives Canada, Ottawa, https://recherche-collection-search.bac-lac.gc.ca/eng/home/record?app=census&IdNumber=22038803&ecopy=e008157833.

2 Michel Lessard, *La nouvelle encyclopédie des antiquités du Québec* (Montreal: Les Éditions de l'Homme, 2007), 334–35.

3 Lessard, *La nouvelle encyclopédie des antiquités du Québec*, 60–61.

4 "Exhibition of Canadian Art," *The Canadian Spectator* 3, no. 18 (May 1, 1880): 210.

5 "Personal," *Hamilton Spectator*, March 8, 1880, 4.

6 George Monro Grant, *Picturesque Canada: The Country as It Was and Is* (Toronto, James Clarke, publisher, 1882), 62.

7 Grant, *Picturesque Canada*, 80, 112.

INDIAN ENCAMPMENT ON THE LOWER ST. LAWRENCE ESTUARY

1 "Ontario Society of Artists. Seventh Annual Exhibition," *Globe*, May 20, 1879, 3.

2 "Academy of Arts," *Globe*, March 9, 1880, 3.

3 Laurier Lacroix, "Montreal and the Origins of the Canadian Academy of Arts," *Vie des arts* 24, no. 98 (1980): 23.

DR. RODDICK'S REMARKABLE CASE OF FAVUS, SHOWING THE DISTRIBUTION OF THE SCABS AND THE EXTENT OF THE ERUPTION ON THE BODY

1 Charles G. Roland, "Osler, Sir William," in *Dictionary of Canadian Biography*, vol. 14 (University of Toronto / Université Laval, 1998), https://www.biographi.ca/en/bio/osler_william_14E.html.

2 As revealed in a letter from William Osler to William Raphael, dated February 7, 1885: "The drawing is lovely but there are one or two points I wish touched up. Dr. Sutherland will take the heart to you and show you. I want the drawing to get off by Thursday Eve to London." Letter quoted in Goelman, "William Raphael," 220.

3 Johann Friedrich Unger, ed., *Reglement für die Akademie der bildenden Künste und mechanischen Wissenschaften zu Berlin* (Berlin, 1790), 20.

4 The letter was transcribed by June Schachter and published in her article "William Osler and William Raphael," Osler Library, McGill University, *Osler Library Newsletter*, nos. 83–84 (1996–97), 2. In the article, she presents two letters signed by the doctor and addressed to William Raphael; both are preserved in the Osler Library archives at McGill University.

5 Schachter, "William Osler and William Raphael," 2. The original drawing of "Atresia of pulmonary artery, with patent Ductus Arteriosus "was preserved in the archives of the Osler Library at McGill University. According to Schachter, the work was signed by Raphael and dated 1878. The author also highlights two other anatomical drawings by William Raphael, dated 1880 and 1882. None of these three drawings could be traced during a search of the archives carried out by staff in 2024 and 2025.

6 William Raphael, *Boy Standing in Profile*, November 14, 1854. From sketchbook no. 2, folio 23r, National Gallery of Canada, Ottawa (inv. 18088.23r).

SAWMILL AND HYDRAULIC DAM

1 Ellen Louise Ramsay, "The Promotion of the Fine Arts in Canada, 1880–1924: The Development of Art Patronage and the Formation of Public Policy" (PhD diss., University College London, 1987), 108–12.

2 Royal Canadian Academy of Arts, *Catalogue of the Exhibition in the Toronto Art Gallery* 7, no. 72 (n.p., 1891).

3 "The Art Exhibition," *Daily Witness*, April 22, 1894, 6.

SIGNIFICANCE & CRITICAL ISSUES

1 Jonathan Wagner, *A History of Migration from Germany to Canada, 1850–1939* (Vancouver: UBC Press, 2006), 22–23.

2 Wagner, *A History of Migration*, 36–39.

3 Wagner, *A History of Migration*, 25.

4 Loren Lerner and Suzanne Rackover, "Jews and Canadian Art," in *Canada's Jews: In Time, Space and Spirit*, ed. Ira Robinson (Boston: Academic Studies, 2013), 422–23.

5 The drawing is preserved at the National Gallery of Canada, Ottawa, in William Raphael's sketchbook no. 2, folio 6v (inv. 18088.6v).

6 Jens Neumann-Schliski, "Un programme commun? Conceptions de l'identité juive dans les Archives israélites et l'Allgemeine Zeitung des Judenthums, 1840–1881," *in Expériences croisées: Juifs de France et d'Allemagne aux XIXe et XXe siècles*, ed. Heidi Knörzer (Paris: Éditions de l'Éclat, 2010), 45.

7 Michael Brown, "The American Connection of Canadian Jews: 1759–1914," *AJS Review* 3 (1978): 60–61.

8 On Abraham de Sola, see Brown, "The American Connection of Canadian Jews," 51-60; Pierre Anctil, *History of the Jews in Quebec* (Ottawa: University of Ottawa Press, 2021), 43–45.

9 Sharon Goelman, "William Raphael, R.C.A. (1833–1914)" (master's thesis, Concordia University, 1978), 44, 140.

10 Goelman, "William Raphael," 41–42, 140, 361, fig. 365.

11 Anctil, *History of the Jews in Quebec*, 35.

12 At most, the artist may have painted himself into *Behind the Bonsecours Market, Montreal*, carrying both a portfolio for his drawings and a candlestick that could be understood as an allusion to his religion. This is the theory suggested by art historian Dennis Reid, *Our Own Country Canada: Being an Account of the National Aspirations of Principal Landscape Artists in Montreal and Toronto 1860–1890* (Ottawa: National Gallery of Canada / National Museums of Canada, 1979), 89.

13 Lerner and Rackover, "Jews and Canadian Art," 423.

14 "Temple Emanu-El Fair," *The Gazette* (Montreal), November 28, 1882, 3; Aline Gubbay, *A View of Their Own: The Story of Westmount* (Montreal: Price-Patterson Ltd., 1998), 73; Goelman, "William Raphael," 255–56n20.

15 "Acknowledgments," *The Gazette* (Montreal), March 11, 1892, 3.

16 "Chanukah Festival," *The Gazette* (Montreal), December 17, 1895, 2.

17 "Chanukah Festival," *The Gazette* (Montreal), 2.

18 John H. Graham, *Outlines of the History of Freemasonry in the Province of Quebec* (Montreal, John Lovell & Son, 1892).

19 Thomas Sargant, *The Freemason's Manual: Containing the First, Second and Third Degrees of Freemasonry* (Toronto: Masonic Publishing Co., 1880), 5.

20 Luc Nefontaine, *La franc-maçonnerie: Une fraternité révélée* (Paris: Découvertes Gallimard, 1994), 44–47.

21 José A. Ferrer Benimeli, "Première condamnation papale, des motivations politiques," *Humanisme* 278, no. 3 (September 2007): 82–83.

22 Goelman, "William Raphael," 44.

23 Goelman, "William Raphael," 45.

24 Édouard Hamon (using the pseudonym Jean D'Erbrée), *La franc-maçonnerie dans la province de Québec en 1883* (n.p., 1883?), 78.

25 Hélène Sicotte, "François Beaucourt (1740–1794) et ses alentours," *Journal of Canadian Art History / Annales d'histoire de l'art canadien* 31, no. 1 (2010): 14–59; Marie-Chantal Leblanc, "Formation artistique et contexte social des peintres canadiens à Paris (1887–1895)" (master's thesis, Université du Québec à Montréal, 2008), 80.

26 Hamon, *La franc-maçonnerie dans la province de Québec*, 64.

27 Hamon, *La franc-maçonnerie dans la province de Québec*, 204.

28 *Proceedings of the Grand Lodge of Ancient and Accepted Masons of Canada at Two Especial Communications Held at the City of Ottawa, Also at Its Twelfth Annual Communication Held at the City of Kingston* (Grand Lodge of Ancient Free and Accepted Masons of Canada, 1867), 386–87. Among the expenses for 1866, we note the payment, on December 29, of $30.50 on behalf of the Grand Lodge of Ancient Free and Accepted Masons of Canada to "W. Notman, for portrait of P.G.M. Simpson."

29 The original portrait of McGillivray, which served as William Raphael's model, is in the McCord Stewart Museum (M18682) and was painted before 1784 by an unknown artist.

30 Pierre B. Landry, "Sandham, Henry," *Dictionary of Canadian Biography*, vol 13 (University of Toronto / Université Laval, 1994), https://www.biographi.ca/en/bio/sandham_henry_13E.html.

31 P. B. Waite, "Campbell, John George Edward Henry Douglas Sutherland, Marquess of Lorne and 9th Duke of Argyll," *Dictionary of Canadian Biography*, vol. 14 (University of Toronto / Université Laval, 2003), https://www.biographi.ca/en/bio/campbell_john_george_edward_henry_douglas_sutherland_14E.html.

32 Moncrieff Williamson, "Harris, Robert," *Dictionary of Canadian Biography*, vol. 14 (University of Toronto / Université Laval, 1998), https://www.biographi.ca/en/bio/harris_robert_14E.html

33 Goelman, "William Raphael," 67–68.

34 "The Art Gallery," *The Gazette* (Montreal), June 5, 1886, 4.

35 "The Art Association," *Daily Witness*, October 15, 1904, 12.

36 I would like to thank Zoë Tousignant for suggesting this line of research during a conversation at the McCord-Stewart Museum in November 2023. I am also grateful to Sharon Goelman for sharing her opinion on this matter in August 2024, which confirmed my research.

37 Michel Tissier, *L'Empire russe en révolutions: Du tsarisme à l'URSS* (Paris: Armand Colin, 2019), 16, 26–27.

38 Richard Pipes, *Russia Under the Old Regime* (New York: Scribner's, 1974).

39 Delphine Diaz, *En exil: Les réfugiés en Europe, de la fin du XVIIIe siècle à nos jours* (Paris: Gallimard, 2021), 155.

40 Anctil, *History of the Jews in Quebec*, 35.

41 Anctil, *History of the Jews in Quebec*, 35.

42 Michael Brown, "Divergent Paths: Early Zionism in Canada and the United States," *Jewish Social Studies* 44, no. 2 (1982): 158.

43 Duncan Bell, *The Idea of Greater Britain: Empire and the Future of World Order, 1860–1900* (Princeton, NJ: Princeton University Press, 2011), 182; Naomi W. Cohen, "American Jewish Reactions to Anti-Semitism in Western Europe, 1875–1900," *Proceedings of the American Academy for Jewish Research* 45 (1978): 52.

44 Alan Mendelson, *Exiles from Nowhere. The Jews and the Canadian Elite* (Montreal, Robin Brass Studio, 2008), 19.

45 Isaac Besht Bendavid, "Goldwin Smith and the Jews," *North American Review* 153, no. 418 (1891): 259.

46 Cohen, "American Jewish Reactions to Anti-Semitism," 32.

47 "A Reply to Beaconsfield," *The Gazette* (Montreal), October 22, 1881, 2; "Goldwin Smith Answered," *New York Times*, November 24, 1881, 6; Bendavid, "Goldwin Smith and the Jews." This anti-Semitism was also felt by Jews in the United States during the same period. See Cohen, "American Jewish Reactions to Anti-Semitism," 36.

48 Goelman, "William Raphael," 71–72.

49 Mendelson, *Exiles from Nowhere*, 2–3.

50 Mendelson, *Exiles from Nowhere*, 2–4.

51 Malcolm Ross, "Goldwin Smith," *Our Living Tradition*, Claude T. Bissell, ed. (Toronto: University of Toronto Press, 1957), 44–45.

52 Goelman, "William Raphael," 88–90.

53 "Eliock School," *The Gazette* (Montreal), July 25, 1893, 5. The announcement is repeated in the same paper on July 26, 1893, as well as on August 14, 23, and 26, 1893. This is probably the institution where he taught Allan J. Hart. See Goelman, "William Raphael," 106.

54 Monique Nadeau-Saumier, "Un espace et un lieu de culture. Le Art Building de Sherbrooke 1887–1927 (PhD diss., Université du Québec à Montréal, 2007), 317–19.

55 "An Art Exhibition of Merit," *Montreal Herald and Daily Commercial Gazette*, 5.

56 As quoted in Goelman, "William Raphael," 100.

57 The plasters were most likely sold, along with thousands of other furniture pieces, objects, and artworks, during sales held by the Sisters of Sainte-Anne between 2019 and 2021. Their current location remains unknown.

58 "An Art Exhibition of Merit," *Montreal Herald and Daily Commercial Gazette*, 5.

59 This work is currently part of Jonathan Wener's collection : William Raphael, *The Habitant*, c.1875, oil on canvas, 26,7 x 20,3 cm, collection Jonathan Wener, Montreal.

60 "An Art Exhibition of Merit," *Montreal Herald and Daily Commercial Gazette*, 5.

61 Raphael's work, *Sunset in Beaurepaire*, was created in 1878 and copied in 1907 by Sister Marie-Hélène-de-la-Croix as *Sunset and Church Steeple*. Both paintings were formerly held at the Sisters of Sainte-Anne Historic Centre.

62 As quoted in Goelman, "William Raphael," 95.

63 "The Art Exhibition," *The Gazette* (Montreal), April 16, 1883, 3.

64 Goelman, "William Raphael," 96.

65 "Art News," *The Gazette* (Montreal), December 17, 1880, 5.

66 Victoria A. Baker, *Scenes of Charlevoix 1784–1950* (Montreal: Musée des beaux-arts de Montréal, 1981), 13–15.

67 "The Fine Arts Bay," *Quebec Daily Mercury*, August 20, 1869, 2.

68 Society of Canadian Artists, *Second Exhibition 1870: Catalogue of Oil and Water Colour Paintings, Exhibited at the Gallery of the Art Association at the Mercantile Library Building, Montreal* (n.p., 1870), 6, no. 57.

69 "Murray Bay," *Montreal Star*, August 20, 1887, 6

70 "Art Education," *The Gazette* (Montreal), December 11, 1880, 3.

STYLE & TECHNIQUE

1 Sharon Goelman, "William Raphael, R.C.A. (1833–1914)" (master's thesis, Concordia University, 1978), 122.

2 Michelle Facos, *An Introduction to Nineteenth Century Art* (New York: Routledge, 2011), 173–75.

3 Geraldine Norman, *Biedermeier Painting 1815–1848: Reality Observed in Genre, Portrait and Landscape* (London: Thames and Hudson, 1987), 8–10.

4 Norman, *Biedermeier Painting*, 8.

5 Norman, *Biedermeier Painting*, 76; Claude Keisch, ed., *The Alte Nationalgalerie Berlin* (London: Scala Publishers, 2005), 53, 56.

6 Marlène Grenier, "Les artistes propagateurs de l'idéal allemand en art pictural et en sculpture au Canada au XIXe siècle" (master's thesis, Université Laval, 1996), 65–66; Norman, *Biedermeier Painting*, 128–29, 142.

7 Mario Béland, "Un peintre allemand à Montréal," *Cap-aux-Diamants*, no. 38 (summer 1994): 65; Grenier "Les artistes propagateurs," 80–81.

8 Mario Béland, "De Berczy à Krieghoff: Peintres étrangers au Bas-Canada 1790–1850," *Vie des Arts* 37, no. 149 (1992): 17.

9 Michel Lessard, *The Livernois, Photographers* (Musée du Québec / Québec Agenda, 1987), 306n27. In his text, the author does not define the links between the photographer and the painter.

10 Norman, *Biedermeier Painting*, 24.

11 The illustration *Rural Bliss*, taken from a special Carnival issue of the *Daily Witness* newspaper, is preserved in the McCord Stewart Museum collection (inv. M979.87.5101.1).

12 Henry Sandham's painting (*Tobogganing, Winter Scene in Montreal*, 1885) is preserved at the National Gallery of Canada, Ottawa (inv. 16642), while Boisseau's work (*La Descente en toboggan*, 1881) is at the Musée national des beaux-arts du Québec, Quebec City (inv. 1980.115).

13 "Art in Continental States", *The Art Journal*, October 1, 1866, 306.

14 "Art in Continental States", 306.

15 The chromolithographs are preserved at the National Archives of Canada, Ottawa (inv. 2878655 and 2878656).

16 "Art in Ottawa," *Montreal Star*, February 6, 1886, 6.

17 "The Art Exhibition," *Montreal Herald and Daily Commercial Gazette*, April 21, 1887, 8.

18 To date, Raphael's *A Difficult Problem* has not been traced.

19 Norman, *Biedermeier Painting*, 129.

20 Norman, *Biedermeier Painting*, 8.

21 "The Fine Arts," *Quebec Daily Mercury*, August 20, 1869, 2.

22 William Raphael was probably the first teacher in Canada to give *plein air* drawing and painting classes. He was a few years ahead of William Brymner, who offered the first such course in 1889 at the Art Association of Montreal. See Jocelyn Anderson, *William Brymner: Life and Work* (Toronto: Art Canada Institute, 2020), 14.

23 "The Art Gallery," *Daily Witness*, April 11, 1883, 8: "The original character in this sketch showed great amusement at having been captured without his knowledge and exhibited by his companion and preceptor."

24 Abbé Jules-Bernardin-Royal Rioux copied William Raphael's work between 1885 and 1895. As Michel Lessard suggests, this is a self-portrait by Rioux. See Michel Lessard, *La nouvelle encyclopédie des antiquités du Québec* (Montreal: Les Éditions de l'Homme, 2007), 498.

25 "The Art Exhibition," *The Gazette* (Montreal), April 16, 1883, 3.

26 The painting was described in the newspaper in 1885. "Our Artists at Work," *Montreal Star*, March 14, 1885, 2.

27 "Art in Canada," *The Gazette* (Montreal), February 6, 1886, 2.

Credits

IMAGE SOURCES

Every effort has been made to secure permissions for all copyrighted material. The Art Canada Institute will gladly correct any errors or omissions.

The Art Canada Institute would like to thank the following for their assistance: Art Gallery of Nova Scotia (Shannon Parker); Art Gallery of Ontario (Alexandra Cousins); Beaverbrook Art Gallery (Dawn Steeves); Bibliothèque et Archives nationales du Québec (Fanny Beaupré, Camille G. Jobin); Bibliothèque des livres rares et collections spéciales de l'Université de Montréal (Éric Bouchard); Château Ramezay (Christine Brisson); Chislehurst Digitization (Jacqueline M.E. Vincent); Congregation Shaar Hashomayim (Hannah Srour-Zackon); Cowley Abbott Fine Art (Julia De Kwant); McCord Stewart Museum (Anne-Frédérique Beaulieu, Christian Vachon); Montreal Museum of Fine Arts (Linda-Anne D'Anjou, Marie-Claude Saia); Musée de la civilisation (Frédérick Bussières); Musée de Lachine (Isabelle Gay, Rose-Laurence Noël); Musée national des beaux-arts du Québec (Julie Bouffard); Musée Pointe-à-Callière (Sophie Bergeron); National Gallery of Canada (Emily Putnam); Rare Books and Special Collections, McGill University Libraries (Jennifer Garland, Ann Marie Holland); RiverBrink Art Museum (Moyu Cheu); Royal Ontario Museum (Nicola Woods); Tom Thomson Art Gallery (Shannon Bingeman); Winnipeg Art Gallery—Qaumajuq (Nicole Fletcher, Sydney Murchison); and Toni Hafkenscheid, Nadine Rose, Dr. Stephenson Strobel, and Jonathan Wener.

The ACI recognizes the additional private collectors who have given permission for their works to be published in this edition.

CREDITS FOR WORKS BY WILLIAM RAPHAEL

An Amateur, 1886. Collection of Jonathan Wener, Montreal. Courtesy of Jonathan Wener.

An Afternoon in the Woods, 1866. Collection of Jonathan Wener, Montreal. Courtesy of Jonathan Wener.

Anatomy Study of Leg Muscles, 1853–57. Collection of the National Gallery of Canada, Ottawa, purchased 1974 (18088.20r). Courtesy of the National Gallery of Canada. Photo credit: NGC.

Arrocher, 1865. Collection of the McCord Stewart Museum, Montreal, gift of Dr. William D. Lighthall (M933.28.1.6). Courtesy of the McCord Stewart Museum.

The Artist's Dog Niny, c.1895. Collection of Jonathan Wener, Montreal. Courtesy of Jonathan Wener.

The Artist's House in Victoria St., 1908. Collection of Jonathan Wener, Montreal. Courtesy of Jonathan Wener.

Awaiting Mother's Return on a Snowy Day, 1891. Collection of Jonathan Wener, Montreal. Courtesy of Jonathan Wener.

Behind Bonsecours Market, Montreal, 1866. Collection of the National Gallery of Canada, Ottawa, purchased, 1957 (6673). Courtesy of the National Gallery of Canada. Photo credit: NGC.

Berlin, 1853, December 11, 1853. Collection of Jonathan Wener, Montreal. Courtesy of Jonathan Wener.

Boating at Dusk, 1878. Collection of Jonathan Wener, Montreal. Courtesy of Jonathan Wener.

The Boating Party, 1876. Collection of the National Gallery of Canada, Ottawa, purchased 1977 (18816). Courtesy of the National Gallery of Canada. Photo credit: NGC.

Bobsledding, Fletcher's Field, Montreal, 1880. Collection of Jonathan Wener, Montreal. Courtesy of Jonathan Wener.

Bonsecours Market, 1864. Private collection. Courtesy of Cowley Abbott. Photo credit: Cowley Abbott.

Bonsecours Market, Montreal, 1880. Collection of the National Gallery of Canada, Ottawa, purchased 2015 (46501). Courtesy of the National Gallery of Canada. Photo credit: NGC.

Boy and a Cart, 1860. Collection of Jonathan Wener, Montreal. Courtesy of Jonathan Wener.

Cap-à-l'Aigle, August 3, 1878. Collection of the National Gallery of Canada, Ottawa, purchased 1974 (18090.29v). Courtesy of the National Gallery of Canada. Photo credit: NGC.

The Coachman, c.1860–1900. Collection of Jonathan Wener, Montreal. Courtesy of Jonathan Wener.

Coachman Standing at Rest Smoking a Pipe, 1881. Collection of Jonathan Wener, Montreal. Courtesy of Jonathan Wener.

Cowansville, July 16, 1885. Collection of the McCord Stewart Museum, Montreal, gift of Dr. William D. Lighthall (M933.27.1.35). Courtesy of the McCord Stewart Museum.

Dam on the St. Charles River, August 11, 1874. Collection of the Musée de Lachine, Montreal, gift of the Sisters of Sainte-Anne (2008.66.13). Courtesy of the Musée de Lachine.

Double Barn Building Reflecting in Water, 1874. Collection of Jonathan Wener, Montreal. Courtesy of Jonathan Wener.

Encampment by the River, 1871. Private collection. Courtesy of Cowley Abbott. Photo credit: Cowley Abbott.

Falaise à Murray Bay, 1887. Collection of Jonathan Wener, Montreal. Courtesy of Jonathan Wener.

Fireside Chat in the Clearing, 1867. Collection of Jonathan Wener, Montreal. Courtesy of Jonathan Wener.

Gathering Wood in Winter, c.1880–1914. Collection of Jonathan Wener, Montreal. Courtesy of Jonathan Wener.

Going to Town, 1862. Samuel E. Weir Collection, RiverBrink Art Museum, Niagara-on-the-Lake, Ontario (982.88). Courtesy of the RiverBrink Art Museum.

Good News, 1875. Collection of Jonathan Wener, Montreal. Courtesy of Jonathan Wener.

Habitant, c.1873–1910. Collection of Jonathan Wener, Montreal. Courtesy of Jonathan Wener.

Habitant at Home, 1873. Collection of Jonathan Wener, Montreal. Courtesy of Jonathan Wener.

Habitant (or *Preparing to Smoke*), c.1872–1910. Collection of Jonathan Wener, Montreal. Courtesy of Jonathan Wener.

Habitant Warming, c.1872–1910. Collection of Jonathan Wener, Montreal. Courtesy of Jonathan Wener.

Habitant with Snowshoes, 1873. Collection of Jonathan Wener, Montreal. Courtesy of Jonathan Wener.

Habitants Attacked by Wolves, 1870. Collection of the Montreal Museum of Fine Arts, gift of the Misses Scott (1923.373). Courtesy of the Montreal Museum of Fine Arts. Photo credit: MMFA.

Half-Breed Fisherman, 1874. Collection of Jonathan Wener, Montreal. Courtesy of Jonathan Wener.

Half-Breed Fisherman, 1877. Collection of Jonathan Wener, Montreal. Courtesy of Jonathan Wener.

Hand on Guitar, January 31, 1854. Collection of the Musée de Lachine, Montreal, gift of the Sisters of Sainte-Anne (2008.62.1). Courtesy of the Musée de Lachine.

Haymarket Square / Victoria Square, 1861. Collection of Jonathan Wener, Montreal. Courtesy of Jonathan Wener.

Head and Figure Studies, 1850–59. Collection of the National Gallery of Canada, Ottawa, purchased 1974 (18091.1). Courtesy of the National Gallery of Canada. Photo credit: NGC.

Indian Encampment on the Lower St. Lawrence Estuary, 1879. Collection of the National Gallery of Canada, Ottawa, Royal Canadian Academy of Arts diploma work, deposited by the artist, Montreal, 1880 (59). Courtesy of the National Gallery of Canada. Photo credit: NGC.

In the Mirror, 1870. Collection of Jonathan Wener, Montreal. Courtesy of Jonathan Wener.

Landscape with Pond and Pink Bushes, August 25, 1885. Collection of Jonathan Wener, Montreal. Courtesy of Jonathan Wener.

William Raphael, *Habitants Attacked by Wolves* (detail), 1870, Montreal Museum of Fine Arts.

Man and Two Women, August 25, 1851. Collection of the National Gallery of Canada, Ottawa, purchased 1974 (18091.12). Courtesy of the National Gallery of Canada. Photo credit: NGC.
Man Posing in a Kneeling Position, c.1851–56. Collection of Jonathan Wener, Montreal. Courtesy of Jonathan Wener.
Man Playing Violin Under Lamppost, 1857. Collection of the National Gallery of Canada, Ottawa, purchased 1974 (18088.11r). Courtesy of the National Gallery of Canada. Photo credit: NGC.
Man Seated, 1886–97. Collection of the National Gallery of Canada, Ottawa, purchased 1974 (18092.23r). Courtesy of the National Gallery of Canada. Photo credit: NGC.
Manuscript of poem entitled *Das Ländliche Leben* (*Life in the Country*), July 6, 1851. Collection of the National Gallery of Canada, Ottawa, purchased 1974 (18091.14). Courtesy of the National Gallery of Canada. Photo credit: NGC.
The McFarlane Children, 1871. Collection of the National Gallery of Canada, Ottawa, gift of Hugh Hanson Davidson, Ottawa, 1987, in memory of C.H. McFarlane (29786). Courtesy of the National Gallery of Canada. Photo credit: NGC.
Moonlight, 1898. Unknown location.
Mr. Sarrasin, St. Gabriel de Brandon (holding pipe), 1872. Collection of Jonathan Wener, Montreal. Courtesy of Jonathan Wener.
Murray Bay, July 30, 1878. Collection of the National Gallery of Canada, Ottawa, purchased 1974 (18090.5r). Courtesy of the National Gallery of Canada. Photo credit: NGC.
Murray Bay Rock in Greenery, 1878. Collection of the Musée de Lachine, Montreal, gift of the Sisters of Sainte-Anne (2008.66.1). Courtesy of the Musée de Lachine.
The Old Pedlar, 1859. Collection of the Art Gallery of Nova Scotia, Halifax, acquired from Lawrence W.B. Morris, 1930 (1930.2). Courtesy of the Art Gallery of Nova Scotia. Photo credit: AGNS.
Old Woman Sitting on Curb, April 23, 1856. Collection of the National Gallery of Canada, Ottawa, purchased 1974 (18088.22r). Courtesy of the National Gallery of Canada. Photo credit: NGC.
Pack of Wolves, c.1879. Collection of the McCord Stewart Museum, Montreal, gift of Dr. Theodore D. Lande (M2002.128.32). Courtesy of the McCord Stewart Museum.
Pointe-au-Pic, Murray Bay—Approaching Storm, 1878. Collection of Jonathan Wener, Montreal. Courtesy of Jonathan Wener.
Portrait of a Habitant in Red Toque, 1906. Collection of Jonathan Wener, Montreal. Courtesy of Jonathan Wener.
Portrait of a Lady, 1884. Collection of the Winnipeg Art Gallery—Qaumajuq, gift of Mr. Peter Dobush (G-65-87). Courtesy of the Winnipeg Art Gallery—Qaumajuq.
Portrait of a Man, 1874. Collection of Jonathan Wener, Montreal. Courtesy of Jonathan Wener.
Portrait of a Woman, June 8, 1855. Collection of the Musée de Lachine, Montreal, gift of the Sisters of Sainte-Anne (2008.63.5). Courtesy of the Musée de Lachine.
Portrait of an Orthodox Jew, 1861. Collection of Jonathan Wener, Montreal. Courtesy of Jonathan Wener.
Portrait of an Orthodox Jew Smoking, 1861. Collection of Jonathan Wener, Montreal. Courtesy of Jonathan Wener.
Portrait of Jeremiah Wright Wilson, 1878. Rare Books and Special Collections Library, University of Montreal, Louis Melzack Canadiana Collection (MZt05). Courtesy of the Galerie de l'Université de Montréal.
Portrait of Louis-Édouard Desjardins, 1877. Collection of Pointe-à-Callière, Montreal Archaeology and History Complex (2018.01.01). Courtesy of Pointe-à-Callière, Montreal Archaeology and History Complex.
Portrait of Mrs. William Raphael, born Ernestina Danziger, December 9, 1891. Collection of Jonathan Wener, Montreal. Courtesy of Jonathan Wener.
Portrait of William McGillivray, 1908. Collection of the Château Ramezay, Montreal. Courtesy of the Château Ramezay.
Portrait of Wolf Rafalsky, c.1880. Collection of Jonathan Wener, Montreal. Courtesy of Jonathan Wener.
The Rafalsky family home in Nakel, May 6, 1851. Collection of the National Gallery of Canada, Ottawa, purchased 1974 (18091.10). Courtesy of the National Gallery of Canada. Photo credit: NGC.
The Rival Beggars, 1861. Collection of Jonathan Wener, Montreal. Courtesy of Jonathan Wener.
Royal Mail, New Brunswick, 1861. Collection of the Beaverbrook Art Gallery, Fredericton, gift of Lord Beaverbrook (1959.176). Courtesy of the Beaverbrook Art Gallery.
Sawmill and Hydraulic Dam, 1889. Collection of Jonathan Wener, Montreal. Courtesy of Jonathan Wener.
Self-Portrait, 1862. Collection of Jonathan Wener, Montreal. Courtesy of Jonathan Wener.
Self-Portrait of the Artist, c.1885. Collection of Jonathan Wener, Montreal. Courtesy of Jonathan Wener.
Shoreline Near Camp, c.1870–1900. Collection of Jonathan Wener, Montreal. Courtesy of Jonathan Wener.
Sinking of the Schooner Industry, December 19, 1856. Collection of Jonathan Wener, Montreal. Courtesy of Jonathan Wener.
Sketchbook No. 3, 1853–76. Collection of the National Gallery of Canada, Ottawa, purchased 1974 (18089.1-36). Courtesy of the National Gallery of Canada. Photo credit: NGC.
Sketch of Hand Writing, 1853–76. Collection of the National Gallery of Canada, Ottawa, purchased 1974 (18089.3). Courtesy of the National Gallery of Canada. Photo credit: NGC.
A Sketch from Nature, October 5, 1882. Collection of Jonathan Wener, Montreal. Courtesy of Jonathan Wener.
Sledding, Fletcher's Field, Montreal, 1875–78. Collection of the National Gallery of Canada, Ottawa, purchased 1974 (18090.19). Courtesy of the National Gallery of Canada. Photo credit: NGC.
Still Life (Northern Flickers), 1885. Collection of the National Gallery of Canada, Ottawa, gift of James G. MacLaren, Ottawa, 2012 (45760). Courtesy of the National Gallery of Canada. Photo credit: NGC.
Still Life with Blossoms, May 24, 1886. Collection of Jonathan Wener, Montreal. Courtesy of Jonathan Wener.
Study after Antinous, 1851–56. Collection of the National Gallery of Canada, Ottawa, purchased 1974 (18088.2v). Courtesy of the National Gallery of Canada. Photo credit: NGC.
Study of a Human Skull, 1851–56. Collection of Dr. Stevenson Strobel, Toronto. Courtesy of Dr. Stevenson Strobel. Photo credit: Toni Hafkenscheid.
Study of a Nude Male Sculpture, 1854. Collection of the National Gallery of Canada, Ottawa, purchased 1974 (18088.3v). Courtesy of the National Gallery of Canada. Photo credit: NGC.
Sunset, n.d. Collection of the Musée de Lachine, Montreal, gift of the Sisters of Sainte-Anne (2008.149). Courtesy of the Musée de Lachine.
Tandem, 1869. Collection of the Musée national des beaux-arts du Québec, Quebec City, purchase (1952.02). Courtesy of the Musée national des beaux-arts du Québec. Photo credit: MNBAQ, Patrick Altman.
Tandem, 1878. Collection of Jonathan Wener, Montreal. Courtesy of Jonathan Wener.
Throwing the Bait, River St. Charles, Quebec, 1895. Private collection. Courtesy of Cowley Abbott. Photo credit: Cowley Abbott.
Two Indian Women, 1873. Collection of the Montreal Museum of Fine Arts, purchase, Museum Campaign Fund (1998-2002). Courtesy of the Montreal Museum of Fine Arts.
Two Women, 1852. Collection of Jonathan Wener, Montreal. Courtesy of Jonathan Wener.
Two Women in Rowboat Near Shoreline, July 5, 1911. Collection of Jonathan Wener, Montreal. Courtesy of Jonathan Wener.
Untitled, 1908. Collection of Jonathan Wener, Montreal. Courtesy of Jonathan Wener.

Untitled (Lake Memphremagog), 1869. Collection of the Tom Thomson Art Gallery, Owen Sound, gift from an anonymous donor through the Ontario Heritage Trust, an agency of the Government of Ontario, 1988 (1988.011.060). Courtesy of the Tom Thomson Art Gallery.

Waiting for the Train, Dunn Station, Lachine, June 25, 1883. Collection of the McCord Stewart Museum, Montreal (M933.27.1.1). Courtesy of the McCord Stewart Museum.

The Walker, 1870. Collection of Jonathan Wener, Montreal. Courtesy of Jonathan Wener.

Where I Was Born—Nakel, Prussia, n.d. Collection of Jonathan Wener, Montreal. Courtesy of Jonathan Wener.

With the Current, 1892. Collection of the Montreal Museum of Fine Arts, purchase, Horsley and Annie Townsend Bequest. Courtesy of the Montreal Museum of Fine Arts. Photo credit: MMFA.

Woman with Dog Sitting on Beach Reading, c.1890–1914. Collection of Jonathan Wener, Montreal. Courtesy of Jonathan Wener.

CREDITS FOR PHOTOGRAPHS AND WORKS BY OTHER ARTISTS

A modest sign on a pilaster in front of 1310 Sainte-Catherine Street, Montreal, indicates William Raphael's studio, c.1884–1910. Photographer unknown. Collection of Jonathan Wener, Montreal.

Aboriginal Bark Huts and Basket Maker, Murray Bay, QC, c.1873, by Livernois Studio. Collection of the McCord Stewart Museum, Montreal, gift of David Watson (MP-1994.26.78). Courtesy of the McCord Stewart Museum.

Antique wooden ark in the sanctuary at the Spanish and Portuguese Synagogue, Montreal, 2018. Photograph by Dave Sidaway / *Montreal Gazette*.

Apollo Belvedere, Drawing Model, second half of the nineteenth century, by an unknown artist, after Leochares. Unknown location.

Art Association Building, Phillips' Square, Montreal, QC, c.1893, by Wm. Notman & Son. Collection of the McCord Stewart Museum, Montreal, purchase, funds graciously donated by *Maclean's* magazine, the Maxwell Cummings Family Foundation, and Empire-Universal Films Ltd. (VIEW-2543.1). Courtesy of the McCord Stewart Museum.

La Banque du Peuple, Montreal, QC, painting by William Raphael, 1872, 1932, by an unknown artist, after William Raphael. Collection of the McCord Stewart Museum, Montreal, gift of George Iles (MP-0000.30.11). Courtesy of the McCord Stewart Museum.

Beaver Hall Hill from Victoria Square, Montreal, QC, 1866, 1866, by William Notman Studio. Collection of the McCord Stewart Museum, Montreal, purchase, funds graciously donated by *Maclean's* magazine, the Maxwell Cummings Family Foundation and Empire-Universal Films Ltd. (I-20928.1). Courtesy of the McCord Stewart Museum.

The Cedar Match, from the Trades, Customs and Legends of Yesteryear series, 1927–31, by Alfred Laliberté. Collection of the Musée national des beaux-arts du Québec, Quebec City, purchase, restoration carried out by the Centre de conservation du Québec (1934.438). Courtesy of the Musée national des beaux-arts du Québec. Photo credit: MNBAQ, Patrick Altman.

Cover of *The Illustrated History of Canada*, edited by Craig Brown (Lester & Orpen Dennys, 1987).

Diploma Pictures—Presented to the New National Gallery, 1880, by unknown artist, in *Grip* 14, no. 18 (March 20, 1880). Courtesy of the National Gallery of Canada. Photo credit: NGC.

Dr. Roddick's Case of Occipital Meningocele, 1880, by John Henry Walker, after William Raphael. Collection of the McCord Stewart Museum, Montreal, gift of David Ross McCord (M930.50.2.161). Courtesy of the McCord Stewart Museum.

Dr. Roddick's Remarkable Case of Favus, Showing the Distribution of the Scabs and the Extent of the Eruption on the Body, 1880, by John Henry Walker, after William Raphael. Collection of the McCord Stewart Museum, Montreal, gift of David Ross McCord (M930.50.2.162). Courtesy of the McCord Stewart Museum.

The Early Bird Picks Up the Worm, 1869, by Roberts & Reinhold, after William Raphael. Collection of Library and Archives Canada, Ottawa. Courtesy of Library and Archives Canada.

Father Moreau (*Le Père Moreau*), 1921, by Marc-Aurèle de Foy Suzor-Coté. Collection of the Musée national des beaux-arts du Québec, purchased in 1927 (1935.52). Courtesy of the Musée national des beaux-arts du Québec. Photo credit: MNBAQ.

Flayed (*Écorché*), 1760, by Edmé Bouchardon. Collection of the École des Beaux-Arts, Paris.

The Gavazzi Riot in Montreal, 1853, by James Duncan. Musée de la civilisation, collection of the Séminaire de Québec, Quebec City. Courtesy of the Musée de la civilisation.

Habitant with Showshoes, 1882, by Edith Cooper, after William Raphael. Published in *Picturesque Canada: The Country as It Was and Is* by George Monro Grant (Toronto: Belden, 1882), volume 1, page 67.

Honoré Mercier, c.1880, by Jules-Ernest Livernois. Collection of Bibliothèque et Archives nationales du Québec, Montreal. Courtesy of Bibliothèque et Archives nationales du Québec.

Hugh Andrew Montagu Allan, Montreal, Quebec, 1866–1867, 1866–67, by the William Notman Studio. Collection of the McCord Stewart Museum, Montreal, gift of Jean-Luc Allard and Lucie Surprenant (M2017.46.2.5139). Courtesy of the McCord Stewart Museum.

Illustrated postcard of Baron de Hirsch School and Institute, Montreal, c.1903–6. Collection of Bibliothèque et Archives nationales du Québec, Montreal. Courtesy of Bibliothèque et Archives nationales du Québec.

In the Orchard (Spring), 1892, by William Brymner. Collection of the National Gallery of Canada, Ottawa, purchased 2002 with the Andrea and Charles Bronfman Canadian Art Fund (41077). Courtesy of the National Gallery of Canada. Photo credit: NGC.

Interior of English, German, and Polish Synagogue on McGill College Avenue, 1890, composite photograph by Rogers Arnott & Sauer. Collection of the Congregation Shaar Hashomayim Museum and Archives, Montreal. Courtesy of the Congregation Shaar Hashomayim Museum and Archives.

Jew's Synagogue, 1839, by James Duncan. Collection of the McCord Stewart Museum, Montreal, gift of Capt. P. Godenrath (M15949.7). Courtesy of the McCord Stewart Museum.

John Wilkes Esq., 1763, by William Hogarth. Collection of the Metropolitan Museum of Art, New York, gift of Sarah Lazarus, 1891 (91.1.8). Courtesy of the Metropolitan Museum of Art.

St. Jean-Baptiste Parade Outside the Montreal Bank, 1872, 1932, by an unknown artist, after William Raphael. Collection of the McCord Stewart Museum, Montreal, gift of George Iles (MP-0000.30.11). Courtesy of the McCord Stewart Museum.

Land of the Lotus Eaters, 1861, by Robert S. Duncanson. Collection of the Royal Palace, Stockholm, Sweden. Courtesy of Wikimedia Commons.

Master Hugh Allan, Montreal, QC, 1867, 1867, by William Notman Studio and John Arthur Fraser (painter). Collection of the McCord Stewart Museum, Montreal, gift of Joan Elspeth Bourne (N-1981.16.1). Courtesy of the McCord Stewart Museum.

Merrymaking, 1860, by Cornelius Krieghoff. Collection of the Beaverbrook Art Gallery, Fredericton, gift of the Beaverbrook Canadian Foundation (1959.120). Courtesy of the Beaverbrook Art Gallery.

Miss Danziger, Montreal, QC, 1862, 1862, by William Notman. Collection of the McCord Stewart Museum, Montreal, purchase, funds graciously donated by *Maclean's* magazine, the Maxwell Cummings Family Foundation, and Empire-Universal Films Ltd. (I-2369.1). Courtesy of the McCord Stewart Museum.

Montmorency Falls, 1853, by Cornelius Krieghoff. Collection of the Art Gallery of Ontario, Toronto, the Tom Thomson Collection at the Art Gallery of Ontario (AGOID.68801). Courtesy of the Art Gallery of Ontario. Photo © AGO.

Niagara Falls, 1869, by Adolphe Vogt. Collection of the National Gallery of Canada, Ottawa, purchased 1965 (14704). Courtesy of the National Gallery of Canada. Photo credit: NGC.

Parade on the Opernplatz, Berlin, 1822, 1829, by Franz Krüger. Collection of the Alte Nationalgalerie, Berlin, acquired in 1928 through a dispute with the former ruling Prussian royal house. Courtesy of the Alte Nationalgalerie.

The Pioneer Mill, 1880, by Homer Watson. Royal Collection Trust, Windsor, acquired by Queen Victoria as a gift from the Marquess of Lorne (RCIN 400548). Photo credit: Royal Collection Trust.

Portrait of Annie McFarlane, 1871, by James Inglis. Collection of the National Gallery of Canada, Ottawa. Courtesy of the National Gallery of Canada. Photo credit: NGC.

Portrait of Jeanie McFarlane, 1871, by James Inglis. Collection of the National Gallery of Canada, Ottawa. Courtesy of the National Gallery of Canada. Photo credit: NGC.

Portrait of William Raphael, c.1911, by Sister Marie-Hélène-de-la-Croix. Collection of the Musée de Lachine, gift of the Sisters of Sainte-Anne. Photo credit: Sisters of Sainte-Anne Historic Centre.

Portrait of William Raphael, c.1865. Photographer unknown. Collection of Jonathan Wener, Montreal. Courtesy of Jonathan Wener.

Prince Consort and Freemasons Group, 1877, 1877, by Notman & Sandham, after James Weston. Collection of the McCord Stewart Museum, Montreal (N-1978.109.22). Courtesy of the McCord Stewart Museum.

The Quebec Tandem Club, Champ De Mars, Montreal, c.1840, by James Duncan. Collection of Royal Ontario Museum, Toronto, gift of Dr. Sigmund Samuel (953.186.1). Courtesy of Royal Ontario Museum.

The Rapids, Montmorency River (*Les Rapides, rivière Montmorency*), 1860, by Otto Reinhold Jacobi. Collection of the Musée national des beaux-arts du Québec, Quebec City, purchase (1936.34). Courtesy of Musée national des beaux-arts du Québec. Photo credit: MNBAQ, Jean-Guy Kérouac.

Right Foot, Drawing Model, second half of the nineteenth century, by an unknown artist. Unknown location.

Sea Trout (*Truites saumonées*), 1893, by Sister Marie-Hélène-de-la-Croix. Collection of the Musée de Lachine, gift of the Sisters of Sainte-Anne (2008.163). Courtesy of the Musée de Lachine. Photo credit: Sisters of Sainte-Anne Historic Centre.

Self-Portrait, 1910, by Robert Harris. Collection of the National Gallery of Canada, Ottawa, purchased 1913 (580). Courtesy of the National Gallery of Canada. Photo credit: NGC.

Shaar Hashomayim Synagogue, 59 McGill College Avenue, Montreal, QC, about 1910–11, c.1910–11, by Wm. Notman & Son. Collection of the McCord Stewart Museum, Montreal, purchase, funds graciously donated by *Maclean's* magazine, the Maxwell Cummings Family Foundation, and Empire-Universal Films Ltd. (VIEW-10763). Courtesy of the McCord Stewart Museum.

Sir Robert Abercromby and W. Dudgeon, Montreal, QC, composite, 1876, 1876, by William Notman Studio. Collection of the McCord Stewart Museum, Montreal, purchase, funds graciously donated by *Maclean's* magazine, the Maxwell Cummings Family Foundation, and Empire-Universal Films Ltd. (II-23851.1). Courtesy of the McCord Stewart Museum.

Sled Race across the Ice, 1861, by Cornelius Krieghoff. Collection of the Montreal Museum of Fine Arts, Lady Allan Bequest (1958.1177). Courtesy of the Montreal Museum of Fine Arts. Photo: MMFA.

The Smoker (*Le Fumeur*), c.1855–60, by Cornelius Krieghoff. Collection of the Musée national des beaux-arts du Québec, Quebec City (1987.202). Courtesy of the Musée national des beaux-arts du Québec. Photo credit: MNBAQ.

"South Kensington Museum: The Sculpture Hall," in *The Queen's London: A Pictorial and Descriptive Record* (London: Cassell & Co., 1896), page 171.

The Steam-ship "Borussia" (screw-propeller). Regular packet between Hamburg and New York, c.1857–72, published by Currier & Ives, New York. Collection of The Mariners' Museum and Park, Newport News, Virginia (1946.0287.000001). Courtesy of The Mariners' Museum and Park.

Study of the Head of an Iroquois Chief, Caughnawaga, 1881, by Georges-Édouard-Amable Desbarats, after William Raphael. McGill Libraries, Rare Books and Special Collections, Montreal. Courtesy of McGill Libraries, Rare Books and Special Collections.

Thomas Douglas Harington, 1850–85, by John Henry Walker. Collection of the McCord Stewart Museum, Montreal, gift of Margaret deVolpi (M982.591.24). Courtesy of the McCord Stewart Museum.

W.H. Simpson, Montreal, QC, 1865, 1865, by William Notman. Collection of the McCord Stewart Museum, Montreal (I-17746.1), purchase, funds graciously donated by *Maclean's* magazine, the Maxwell Cummings Family Foundation and Empire-Universal Films Ltd. (I-17705.1). Courtesy of the McCord Stewart Museum.

William Brymner with his students at the Art Association of Montreal, 1902. Photographer unknown. Jean-Marie Gauvreau Fonds, Centre de conservation, Bibliothèque et Archives nationales du Québec, Montreal (MSS-002). Courtesy of the Musée national des beaux-arts du Québec, Quebec City.

William Raphael, artist, Montreal, QC, 1862, 1862, by William Notman. Collection of the McCord Stewart Museum, Montreal, purchase, funds graciously donated by *Maclean's* magazine, the Maxwell Cummings Family Foundation, and Empire-Universal Films Ltd (I-2362.1). Courtesy of the McCord Stewart Museum.

William Raphael, painter, c.1890. Photographer unknown. Collection of the McCord Stewart Museum, Montreal, gift of David Ross McCord (MP-0000.2596). Courtesy of the McCord Steward Museum.

William Raphael in his studio, c.1905. Photographer unknown. Collection of Jonathan Wener, Montreal. Courtesy of Jonathan Wener.

William Raphael's painting palette, c.1879–1914. Collection of the Musée de Lachine, gift of the Sisters of Sainte-Anne (2009.159.17). Courtesy of the Musée de Lachine. Photo credit: Sisters of Sainte-Anne Historic Centre.

William Raphael, *Bonsecours Market* (detail), 1864, private collection.

William Raphael, *Untitled*, 1908, watercolour on paper, 15.2 x 20.3 cm, collection of Jonathan Wener, Montreal.

Acknowledgements

The Art Canada Institute gratefully acknowledges the generosity of Power Corporation of Canada, Season Sponsor, 2025–2026 Publications. A heartfelt thank you to the sponsors of this publication: Presenting Sponsor: Jonathan Wener, CM; Title Sponsors: Alan and Patricia Koval Foundation, The Schulich Foundation, and The Jack Weinbaum Family Foundation; Gold Sponsor: The Morris & Rosalind Goodman Family Foundation; Silver Sponsors: The Azrieli Foundation, The Delaney Family Foundation, The DH Gales Family Charitable Foundation, and The Spatz Foundation; Contributors: Tamara Fine and Darren Sukonick, Peter and Neri Slan, and The Weisz Family.

From the Author

A fuller picture of William Raphael's work extends far beyond the limited holdings in museums and public collections, thanks to the dedication of his great-great-grandson, Jonathan Wener. Though not an artist himself, Wener has shaped Montreal's urban landscape through Canderel, the real-estate firm he founded in 1975, and has long applied the same vision and care to preserving Raphael's legacy. Over decades, he has acquired, restored, and safeguarded a remarkable number of his ancestor's works, creating an invaluable reference collection that reflects both his sensitivity as a collector and his commitment to stewarding a shared family and public heritage. His generous support—granting unlimited access to this collection and encouraging sustained research—has made this Art Canada Institute publication possible, ensuring Raphael's life and art can be more widely known.

I am indebted to many people for their assistance in preparing this book. The invitation to explore the work and life of William Raphael came from Annie Gérin, dean of the Faculty of Fine Arts at Concordia University. I sincerely thank her for her trust and for introducing me to the team at the Art Canada Institute and its executive director and founder, Sara Angel. With her support and the collaboration of many professionals at ACI, including Emma Doubt, Victoria Nolte, Tara Ng, Annie Champagne, Simone Wharton, and Philip Dombowsky, this project has become a reality. To all of them, I offer my deepest gratitude.

My thanks also go to the many institutions and staff members of various departments with whom I corresponded for my research. I would especially like to thank Christian Vachon (McCord Stewart Museum), Nadine Rose (Wener Family Office), Emmy Côté (Collège de Maisonneuve), Mathieu Tremblay, Rose-Laurence Noël (Musée de Lachine), Anne Whitelaw (Concordia University), Mary-Dailey Desmarais, Clarence Epstein, Sal Guerrera, Craig Klinkhoff, and the Alan Klinkhoff Gallery for their valuable contributions to this project.

I would also like to acknowledge the assistance of Ulrike Möhlenbeck (Akademie Der Künste Archiv, Berlin); Troy Wagner (Art Gallery of Nova Scotia); Christine Brisson (Château Ramezay); Éric Bouchard (Library of Rare Books and Special Collections, Université de Montréal); Myriam Barriault Fortin (Galerie de l'Université de Montréal); Dominic Hardy (Université du Québec à Montréal); Zoë Tousignant and Heather McNabb (McCord Stewart Museum); Nathalie Galego, Julie Alary Lavallée, and Renée Filbey (Musée d'art de Joliette); Jacques Des Rochers and Danielle Blanchette (Montreal Museum of Fine Arts); Daniel Drouin (Musée national des beaux-arts du Québec); Asta McCann (RiverBrink Art Museum); Carol Baum (Royal Ontario Museum); Sonya Jones (Robert McLaughlin Gallery); Shannon Bingeman (Tom Thomson Art Gallery); Sydney Murchison (Winnipeg Art Gallery); Sharon Goelman; and Mario Béland. I am deeply grateful to them for granting me access to both the artworks and useful information for this book.

William Raphael, *Shoreline Near Camp*, c.1870–1900, oil on canvas, 30.5 x 43.2 cm, collection of Jonathan Wener, Montreal.

About the Author

William Raphael's arrival in Montreal in 1857 provides insight into the conditions that influenced the integration of Jewish artists into a cultural milieu that was still in the making. It is no small feat that Raphael was able to contribute so profoundly to Quebec's visual folklore, while also receiving praise for his depictions of rural life and modern urban reality. — PIERRE-OLIVIER OUELLET

Pierre-Olivier Ouellet is an art historian and professor at Cégep du Vieux Montréal. He holds a PhD from Rennes 2 University in France, where he studied the art collections of laypeople under the French regime. He is interested in various aspects of artistic production in Canada before 1900, such as the representation of Indigenous peoples, artistic works related to missionary activities, the history of materials and techniques, art after the Conquest, and art historiography. The author of several scholarly essays, he has published in Quebec and Europe, notably in exhibition catalogues and books, including *François-Marc Gagnon et l'art au Québec: Hommage et parcours* (Montreal: Presses de l'Université de Montréal, 2021), *L'homme des bois, l'homme vert: L'imaginaire de l'homme sylvestre dans la littérature et les arts* (Rennes: Presses universitaires de Rennes, 2019), *Trading Paintings and Painters' Materials 1550–1800* (London: Archetype Publications, 2019), *Le fabuleux destin des tableaux des abbés Desjardins: Peintures des XVIIe et XVIIIe siècles des musées et églises du Québec* (Ghent: Snoeck, 2017), and *Québec: Une ville et ses artistes* (Quebec: Musée national des beaux-arts du Québec, 2008). Ouellet's articles have also appeared in several academic journals, including *Legatio: The Journal for Renaissance and Early Modern Diplomatic Studies* (vol. 4, 2020), *IKON: Journal of Iconographic Studies* (vol. 12, 2019), *Bulletin d'histoire politique* (vol. 26, no. 1, 2017), and the *Revue de Bibliothèque et Archives nationales du Québec* (no. 3, 2011). Very active in teaching and research, he is currently exploring the work of artist and architect François Baillairgé (1759–1830), studying the iconic painting *La France apportant la foi aux Wendat de la Nouvelle-France*, c.1666, and investigating the writings of art historian Gérard Morisset (1898–1970), all while continuing to explore lesser-known or less-appreciated works of art in Quebec and Canadian history.

William Raphael
Life & Work

This book is part of the Canadian Art Library Series, published by the Art Canada Institute.

Art Canada Institute
Massey College, University of Toronto
4 Devonshire Place
Toronto, ON M5S 2E1

Library and Archives Canada Cataloguing in Publication

Title: William Raphael : life & work / by Pierre-Olivier Ouellet.
Other titles: William Raphael. English
Names: Ouellet, Pierre-Olivier, 1978- author. | Container of (work): Raphael, William, 1833-1914.
Paintings. Selections. | Art Canada Institute, publisher.
Description: Translation of: William Raphael : sa vie et son œuvre.
Identifiers: Canadiana (print) 20250174383 | Canadiana (ebook) 20250174324 | ISBN 9781487103774 (hardcover) | ISBN 9781487103736 (HTML) | ISBN 9781487103750 (PDF)
Subjects: LCSH: Raphael, William, 1833-1914. | LCSH: Raphael, William, 1833-1914—Criticism and interpretation. | LCSH: Painters—Canada—Biography. | LCGFT: Biographies.
Classification: LCC ND249.R34 O9413 2025 | DDC 759.11—dc23

Printed in Belgium.

IMAGE CREDITS

COVER

William Raphael, *Bonsecours Market, Montreal*, 1880, oil on canvas, 30.4 x 40.7 cm, National Gallery of Canada, Ottawa. (See fig. 25.)

HALF TITLE PAGES

[1] William Raphael, *Sketch of Hand Writing*, 1853–76, graphite on wove paper, 10.5 x 16.8 cm, National Gallery of Canada, Ottawa.
[2] William Raphael, *Two Indian Women*, 1873, oil on paper mounted on cardboard, 25 x 18.1 cm, Montreal Museum of Fine Arts. (See fig. 146.)
[3] William Raphael, *Haymarket Square / Victoria Square*, 1861, oil on canvas, 51.1 x 63.5 cm, collection of Jonathan Wener, Montreal. (See fig. 60.)
[4] William Raphael, *Tandem*, 1869, oil on canvas, 56.5 x 92.3 cm, Musée national des beaux-arts du Québec, Quebec City. (See fig. 69.)
[5] William Raphael, *Behind Bonsecours Market, Montreal*, 1866, oil on canvas, 67.5 x 109.6 cm, National Gallery of Canada, Ottawa. (See fig. 63.)

TITLE PAGE AND BACK COVER IMAGE

William Raphael, *Self-Portrait of the Artist*, c.1885, oil on canvas, 61 x 50.8 cm, collection of Jonathan Wener, Montreal. (See fig. 113.)

SPONSORSHIP PAGE

William Raphael, *Woman with Dog Sitting on Beach Reading*, c.1890–1914, oil on canvas, 30.5 x 43.2 cm, collection of Jonathan Wener, Montreal.

TABLE OF CONTENTS

William Raphael, *The Boating Party*, 1876, oil on canvas, 33.2 x 52.4 cm, National Gallery of Canada, Ottawa. (See fig. 95.)

CHAPTER OPENERS

[Biography] William Raphael, painter, c.1890, photographer unknown, McCord Stewart Museum, Montreal. (See fig. 108.)
[Key Works] William Raphael, *With the Current*, 1892, oil on canvas, 40.8 x 63.5 cm, Montreal Museum of Fine Arts. (See fig. 94.)
[Significance & Critical Issues] William Raphael, *Boy and Cart*, 1860, oil on canvas, 58.4 x 47 cm, collection of Jonathan Wener, Montreal. (See fig. 19.)
[Style & Technique] William Raphael, *Pointe-au-Pic, Murray Bay—Approaching Storm*, 1878, oil on cardboard, 28.3 x 45.5 cm, collection of Jonathan Wener, Montreal. (See fig. 34.)
[Sources & Resources] William Raphael, *Coachman Standing at Rest Smoking a Pipe*, 1881, oil on canvas, 50.8 x 40.6 cm, collection of Jonathan Wener, Montreal. (See fig. 38.)

BOOK CREDITS

PUBLISHER
Sara Angel

COMMISSIONING EDITOR
Victoria Nolte

EXECUTIVE EDITOR
Tara Ng

EDITOR
Annie Champagne

BOOK DESIGNER
Simone Wharton

COPY EDITOR AND PROOFREADER
Janice Weaver

IMAGE RESEARCHER
Philip Dombowsky

PRINTING
Type A Print